Couple Therapy Workbook

Resolve conflicts and build deep connections before your relationship falls

Natalia Crimson

© Copyright 2018 Natalia Crimson - All rights reserved.

The content contained within this book may not be reproduced, duplicated or transmitted without direct written permission from the author or the publisher.

Under no circumstances will any blame or legal responsibility be held against the publisher, or author, for any damages, reparation, or monetary loss due to the information contained within this book, either directly or indirectly.

Legal Notice:

This book is copyright protected. It is only for personal use. You cannot amend, distribute, sell, use, quote or paraphrase any part, or the content within this book, without the consent of the author or publisher.

Disclaimer Notice:

Please note the information contained within this document is for educational and entertainment purposes only. All effort has been executed to present accurate, up to date, reliable, complete information. No warranties of any kind are declared or implied. Readers acknowledge that the author is not engaged in the rendering of legal, financial, medical or professional advice.

The content within this book has been derived from various sources. Please consult a licensed professional before attempting any techniques outlined in this book.

By reading this document, the reader agrees that under no circumstances is the author responsible for any losses, direct or indirect, that are incurred as a result of the use of the information contained within this document, including, but not limited to, errors, omissions, or inaccuracies.

Table of Contents

Table of Contents

Introduction...**6**

Chapter 1 ....**8**

- ❖ Communication Guidelines
  - Communication Ground
  - Rules Designing Your Own Rules

Chapter 2 ....**33**

- ❖ Setting the Mood

Chapter 3 ....**44**

- ❖ The "Obvious" Questions
  - The "Ultimates" List
  - Perceptions:
  - How We See Ourselves and Each Other
  - Describing Yourself
  - What Your Partner Sees in You
  - Comparing and Contrasting Perceptions of Shared Experience

Chapter 4..**59**

- ❖ The "Little" Questions
  - The Devil is in the Details
  - The "Little" Questions — Preferences and Personality

- More "Little" Questions — Experience and Emotion

Chapter 5 76
- ❖ The "Big Picture" Questions
  - Miracle Questions
  - Ranking Priorities
  - Values

Chapter 6 89
- ❖ The "Past" Questions
  - Attachment Theory
  - Your Childhood
  - Relationship History

Chapter 7 107
- ❖ The "Future" Questions
  - "Where are we headed as individuals? "
  - "Where are we headed as a couple?"
  - Maintaining the Self in a Partnership

Chapter 8 123
- ❖ The "Touchy" Questions
  - Communication Guidelines for Ideological Disputes
  - Personal Sensitivities
  - The Broken Record

- The "Touchy" Questions
- Putting Theory into
- Practice Moving Forward

Chapter 9...**137**

❖ <u>The "Touchy Feely" Questions</u>
- Enjoying Emotional Intimacy
- Improving Physical Intimacy

Chapter 10 ....**143**

❖ <u>Maintaining the Magic</u>
- Brainstorming New Activities Together
- Get Your Heart Racing
- "What makes us work?"
- Creating a Connection Ritual

Conclusion..**166**

Introduction

The following chapters will provide you with useful insights into what makes any romantic partnership successful and satisfying; furthermore, it will arm you with a number of strategies, tools, questionnaires, and quizzes to discover, pursue, and realize your personal relationship goals. You'll find guided questions to help you learn more about yourself, your partner, the unique relationship you share, and how to keep it thriving for many years to come.

This book was designed with the intention of making the concepts of couples' therapy accessible to those who cannot find the time, money, or transport to reach a therapist's office. It also aims to make this work as simple, easy, and enjoyable as possible. Some chapters may pose challenging questions that expose difficulties in your relationship, while many others will offer fun, stress-free interactive exercises that you'll want to incorporate into date nights or lazy weekend mornings together.

The concepts included can be applied to any relationship, whether your partnership is weeks, months, years, or decades old. You'll find activities designed for couples to use together, but you'll also find questionnaires to complete on your own which will help you to clarify your goals, both as an individual and as half of a partnership. This is a great book to keep handy at your bedside table or to carry with you and squeeze in a few minutes of relationship work wherever and whenever you can find time.

There are plenty of books on this subject on the market, so thank you again for choosing this one! Every effort was made to ensure it is full of as much useful information as possible, please enjoy!

Chapter 1

Communication Guidelines

It may seem obvious to you that good communication is the foundation of every healthy, functioning relationship. All romantic connections are built, in essence, on physical attraction and discourse; and while physical attraction is a mysterious science, requiring the cooperation of good timing, good lighting, hormones, and perhaps even the correct alignment of celestial bodies, communication is an aspect of our relationship that is always entirely in our hands. At any time or place, in the company of any person, we can strive to do better with our words, tone, and body language. No matter what external factors may perturb or distract us, we can practice better-listening habits. Though we cannot control what happens to us, we can always control our reactions. We can shape the world around us through becoming better communicators, learning how to ask for the reactions we want, avoid unnecessary confusion, and manage any conflicts that may arise.

Good communication skills will positively impact all of the relationships in your life, but this book will focus primarily on the practices that will have the greatest impact on the unique bond you share with your partner. You can aim to use these tools throughout your personal life, with friends and co-workers and family members--but regardless of how you incorporate these ideas into your day-to- day life, you and your partner should make a concerted effort to use these skills as you complete any of the questionnaires, quizzes or activities you find in this book. You may find a number of the questions to be challenging or provocative--they are intended to be! But you will find that with a toolbox of positive communication skills and a game plan to handle conflict, even the most nerve-wracking discussions will become manageable with your partner.

Perhaps they'll even become easy and comfortable, once you are well- practiced with these skills.

It's recommended that both partners read this chapter on communication, as well as chapter two, before diving into any workbook activities. If your partner isn't able to read these chapters, you can instead ask them to share a conversation about what you've learned. You may also want to review the questions at the end of this chapter with your partner in order to tailor the communication skills outlined here to your unique personalities. Some rules for effective communication can be applied with a one-size-fits-all mentality, while others may need to be altered to suit the individuals in question.

Now, let's communicate!

I could start you off with some of the same basics of good communication you'd find in any book about improving your relationship--how to make eye contact and be an active listener, how to use "I feel" statements and avoid pointing the finger of blame at your partner, and so on. But since you purchased this book rather than the others, let me start with a concept that might strike you as somewhat radical, and then together, we can work backward to see how this theory works in practice.

Ready? Braced yourself? Okay, here we go. Disagreements do not have to be conflicts.

And furthermore, conflicts don't have to become fights.

If you're lucky, this idea may not be too difficult for you to swallow. Many of us display a firm grasp on this concept with people who don't hold too large a piece of our hearts in their hands; we are often able to disengage from unproductive or antagonistic interactions with strangers or acquaintances, choosing to shrug our shoulders and say: "This isn't worth getting riled over." Most of us are quite young when we first hear the phrase "pick your battles," and since the concept is so familiar, we assume that we have mastered it, more or less, by the time we reach adulthood.

Since communication is something we learn as small children, and use pretty much every day of our lives, it's easy to take our own communication habits for granted. As any relationship, whether romantic, platonic, familial or professional, grows over time, we eventually become blinded to the nuanced ways in which we develop communicative cultures with one another. This means to say we may not be conscious of the fact that we use a different tone of voice when speaking to our significant other versus our parent, friend, boss, or clerk behind the counter at the corner store. We may not notice that we always use "pleases," "thank yous" and "excuse mes" with strangers and colleagues, while rarely extending the same courtesies to those we spend the most time with. We might not be aware that we exude positivity to our friends while wallowing in negative emotions behind closed doors with our loved ones. Most importantly, we may not recognize that we use a different set of rules in communicating with our partners than those we use with other people.

The first step in becoming a better communicator is finding the will to self-reflect. Are you mindful of where your eyes are focused when you speak to your partner, your boss, your grocery clerk? Does the pitch of your voice change when you are excited, distracted, stressed, or comfortable? How loud or quiet are you? And does this change in varied environments? In conversations, do you ask a lot of questions, or talk about yourself more? What do you do with your hands, mouth, eyes, while you're listening? How deliberate is your communication behavior?

Whether you come to recognize your own behaviors by simply making an effort to further your self-awareness, or you need direct feedback from others, you'll probably encounter a few moments of discomfort, and the impulse to become defensive or dismissive. You

may feel compelled to say something along the lines of: "Well, that's just the way I am! I can't help it!"

When those feelings come, try to take a deep breath, maybe even close your eyes, and remind yourself that nothing about your behavior or personality is set in stone. Even if you are a generally cynical person, you do have the ability to control when you smile or scowl.

You can control the volume of your voice, the tension in your shoulders; you can choose to gesticulate or cross your arms or keep your hands stuffed in your pockets. The first step to being a better communicator is being willing to see yourself without denial or a defensive reaction. The second step is to embrace the notion that in every interaction, under any set of circumstances, your behavior is your choice. Your reactions are not predetermined like muscular reflexes. There are always options.

Here's another radical notion to embrace: some conflicts are impossible to avoid and for good reason.

Sometimes, fights can be good for a relationship.

Of course, we usually don't feel that way in the throes of a disagreement. Intense, antagonistic conflict creates physical symptoms in our bodies which can sometimes last long after our rational minds have declared the fight to be over. If you experience these symptoms repeatedly in the company of another person, your body will eventually start to persuade you to spend less time around them for the sake of your own well-being.

This is why practicing good communication--both during times of conflict and at points when everything seems to be running smoothly--is paramount for a healthy relationship.

Conflicts don't usually arise because one of you is looking for a fight. Often, they seem to come out of nowhere; you're trying to decide what to eat for dinner, or which movie to see this weekend or what color rug would look best in your living room, when suddenly, someone perceives offense where none was intended, and ten minutes later, you're yelling and crying and trading insults.

These types of arguments are rarely about the trigger that sparked them. Your rational brain may know, for instance, that even if chocolate is your absolute favorite food in the universe, that doesn't mean others will feel the same way about it; furthermore, your rational brain may understand that you don't stand to lose anything when your partner declares that chocolate is repulsive. In fact, you stand to gain something--more chocolate for you, plus now you know something new about your significant other! Yet somehow, at the moment, your inability to agree on a matter of taste feels like a real problem and overshadows all the things that you do agree on.

Often, these types of disagreements can spiral into more serious arguments when we fail to recognize boundaries.

For one, we fail to remember that there is a boundary between the self and the chocolate in question-- meaning, just because we love something fully, that doesn't mean it is a part of us. Your partner's rejection of your favorite food is not the same as a rejection of who you are. It may also be a struggle to recognize the boundary between yourself and your loved one; as two unique individuals, you don't need to agree on everything.

Furthermore, we sometimes fail to recognize the boundary between the disagreement and a bigger unspoken issue that it represents. For instance, if you happen to express your love for others through baking, then differing opinions on the taste of chocolate may mean more to you than just switching to oatmeal raisin cookies. It may echo a deeper fear that your loving feelings have been lost in translation, or that you and your partner don't want the same things out of life.

If this has been a repeated cycle in your relationship, please rest assured: this happens to everyone, even those who are deeply compatible and committed to one another. Still, even if this kind of interaction doesn't mean you'll need to end the relationship, it does indicate that one or both of you need to work on your communication skills.

Practiced healthy communicators can avoid placing blame and aim not to take things personally. They can appreciate the differences they note between themselves and others and consider their own feelings before they react to external stimulus. A well- practiced communicator might resolve the conflict above by saying: "Listen, it doesn't really matter if we agree about chocolate or not. But this has led me to question whether or not we're on the same page about a few more important issues, and I'm feeling insecure about that. Can we try to talk this out?"

If you can communicate more effectively before arguments come up, you'll have fewer bottled-up issues to bring to the table, so you'll be less likely to explode. You'll have more established common ground with your partner, and thus find it easier to work together towards a resolution, instead of going around in circles playing the blame game. In other words, you'll find it less exhausting to fight together for the sake of the relationship, rather than fighting against each other so that one of you might come out on top. And finally, if you can use positive communication skills during an argument, you'll be able to effectively express your frustrations and unmet needs without causing unnecessary hurt or shame in your partner.

Fights can be good for us when they accomplish something positive in the end, precipitating necessary change in ways that calm, healthy discussions rarely do. You and your partner may stumble into a disagreement about something more serious than chocolate - say, for example, that you are not terribly fond of your partner's best friend from work, and the weekly dinners you share with this friend are starting to drive you nuts. It would be difficult for any couple to handle this issue without conflict, but if you are able to manage the conflict in a healthy way, the fight may be worthwhile. You might both realize that you don't need to attend these dinners anymore, while your partner can continue to spend quality time with friends. Removing yourself from these dinners should ultimately serve to put less strain on your relationship, and maybe even allow you to appreciate your shared time more than you previously did.

If a conclusion can be reached without either person blaming, shaming, insulting or manipulating the other, then call it a "good" fight--a necessary, though difficult, conversation that works to facilitate positive change. When it's over, go ahead and congratulate each other--if good fights were easy to stage, everyone would have them.

Communication Ground Rules

Here are some universal ground rules to facilitate better communication, in any circumstance. Review these with your partner before diving into questionnaires, or whenever tensions arise between you.

Focus on listening

If you and your partner have been struggling to connect or understand one another, it may be helpful for each of you to treat any serious discussion like a school-assigned book report. While you listen, pretend that there will, in fact, be a quiz later on to evaluate how much you understood. When you're silent only because you're brainstorming what to say next and waiting for your turn to speak, it shows. Instead, start by aiming to display how well you've understood what your partner just said before moving on. Say something like: "Okay, I think what I just heard you say was…" and then rephrase their sentiments in your own words. If your understanding misses the mark, allow your partner the opportunity to explain their perspective again.

Everyone appreciates being well-heard, so this is one of the simplest and easiest ways to endear a person to you, even amid an argument.

Share the floor

Have you ever been on the receiving end of a conversation with someone who wouldn't let you get a word in edgewise? If so, you know how unpleasant it can be. In romance, it's good to talk about ourselves, and exude a certain degree of bravado, as confidence and self-esteem can be quite attractive. Still, try to be conscious of how much your partner is contributing to any discussion you share. They may be a generally quiet person; perhaps you're more of an extrovert, while your partner tends to stay tight-lipped. Even so, it

isn't a bad idea to check in with them from time to time. Ask your partner what they think of the matter at hand, or even if they'd like the change the subject. They may decline to speak, telling you they have nothing to say and no desire to change the conversation topic, but they will be happy to know that their opinion matters to you, nonetheless.

If interruption is an issue in your relationship, particularly during disagreements, both parties should make an effort to nip this habit in the bud. Interruptions leave us feeling disrespected and unheard. Instead, make a pact between both of you.

When one person interrupts the other, stop them right away, saying, "Can I please finish what I'm saying?" and then continue with your thought. On the other hand, if you find you need to interrupt to get a word in edgewise with your partner, make a practice of doing so respectfully. "May I say something, please?" or "I'd appreciate the chance to contribute, here," are both examples of gentle interruptions. If either of you finds it difficult to respect this agreement, it may be necessary to disengage from the conversation for a short while until tempers cool.

Use "I feel" statements

This tool can help you to strengthen your boundaries subconsciously, through the psychology of the language used. When we use the words "I feel" to express our desires or frustrations, we take personal responsibility for our own emotions. It is difficult to leave your partner feeling blamed, attacked, or vilified when you use this language because you frame the statement as a piece of your personal perspective, rather than an objective truth. This language can also help to pinpoint where your wires are getting crossed in repeated arguments because couples can quibble endlessly over what is or isn't true, but it's difficult to disagree with another person's emotions.

Avoid absolutes and extremes

Using extreme language is a surefire way to put any disagreement on the fast track to an explosive conflict. We all feel the impulse to defend ourselves from any attack, whether it is warranted or not. When an attack comes in the form of an extreme accusation-- "You never do the dishes!" or "You're always interrupting me!" or "You're the worst at remembering special occasions!" -- people tend to dispute the absolute parts of the sentence while ignoring the real substance of the conflict.

It would be easy to fall into a defensive mode, arguing that you have in fact done the dishes a few times, you do not actually interrupt every single one of your partner's sentences, and you did manage to remember an anniversary three years ago, thus concluding that it's your partner who's truly in the wrong here.

Adding words like "never," "always," "best," "worst," "forever," "most," "least," to a sentence can actually weaken our statements since these absolutes are rarely true or realistic.

Also, using absolutes can lead others to hear things we aren't saying; to some ears, the phrase "you never do the dishes" might sound a whole lot like "you are selfish," "you are lazy," "you are incompetent," or, in a worst case scenario, it might sound like: "

You possess an innate, fundamental character flaw, and there is no hope for your redemption."

By being more careful and precise with our language, we can more easily get to the bottom of the problem. "You never do the dishes" will quickly leave the accused feeling the need to prove their moral virtues or defend their human fallibility, but saying "It would really mean a lot to me if you'd help with the dishes more often," invites them to work towards a solution without feeling shamed.

Resist the urge to make assumptions

This can be especially challenging for those in long-term relationships. After years together, you come to know so much about your significant other that you may start to see them as an extension of yourself. But even if you've shared a home with your partner for

decades, there is always a chance that they'll surprise you. People grow, evolve, and change in unpredictable ways.

Give your partner the opportunity to confound your expectations. Try not to presume disappointment, annoyance, jealousy, anger or apathy.

Ask your partner: "How do you feel about this?" Generally speaking, we humans love to talk about ourselves in low-pressure situations; this is why it's fun and amusing to tell your friends about an embarrassingly bad job interview you stumbled through, but mortifying to actually sit through the interview in question. If you want to encourage honesty in your partner, express curiosity and keep things low-pressure by making it clear that you're open to whatever answer they might give you.

Respect the contextual environment

We'll delve deeper into this in the next chapter, but as a general rule, it's important to note that healthy communication can only occur in places and times where both parties are free to engage. You can use "I feel" statements all day long with your partner, but if he or she is overstressed by work, running late against a deadline, grieving a major loss, inebriated, overtired, sick or injured, it's not likely that they'll be able to meet you halfway. This skill requires that we connect and empathize with our partner purposefully. Make an effort to learn more about your partner's daily schedule, sources of stress, and personal physical needs. I, for one, cannot contribute to any productive conversation before I've had a full cup of coffee; since my partner came to terms with this reality a few years back, we haven't had a single early morning disagreement.

Know when to call a time-out

During any deep emotional discussion or conflict, it's important to recognize the role that stamina plays in communication. Some people find emotional vulnerability exhausting; others can become quickly exasperated by repetitive cycles in a conversation. Despite your best efforts to use healthy communication strategies, there may

come to a point when you have to admit to yourselves that the conversation isn't going anywhere productive.

Give yourself permission to take short breaks. Generally, you should aim to repair conflicts in the relationship quickly so there won't be a lot of time for resentments to fester and grow. But sometimes, it's better to take a hiatus for an hour, or full a day, and prevent yourself from saying something in the heat of the moment that you won't be able to take back, rather than to stay and allow the conflict to continue escalating.

These are signs that you might need to take a walk and get some space to think: elevated heartbeat or other physical anxiety symptoms; circular conversations; name-calling, harsh insults, or displays of disrespect; physical outbursts; high-stakes and ultimatums.

Be mindful of the fact that breaks need to be mutually agreed upon. Storming out in the middle of an argument is not productive, and will usually just leave you with one more thing to disagree over.

Designing Your Own Rules

One of the most enjoyable parts of emotional intimacy with a partner is the ability to share inside jokes, pet names, obscure references, and unique rituals--this is what some relationship coaches might call your "relationship culture." It is almost as if you and your partner have created your own dialect of a language, which only the two of you can truly understand. This is part of the reason that we fear the endings of relationships despite having rational reasons to call it quits; it's not just a fear of losing the person, but furthermore, a fear of losing access to the entire inner world we've built with them.

This being the case, it may feel awkward or unusually formal, at first, to practice using these communication skills with your loved one. You're comfortable together, so introducing any kind of script to your interactions will feel unnatural and inauthentic initially. With practice over time, these behaviors will feel less forced, but there are also some tricks you can use to minimize the discomfort immediately.

Suppose, for instance, that your significant other doesn't want to use "I feel" statements; perhaps this person had a horrible experience in family therapy as a child, and this terminology immediately puts them in a defensive or apathetic mood. If you both share the common goal of improving communication, there is no reason in the world why you couldn't agree on a turn of phrase that suits you better and accomplishes the same objective.

Here are some questions you can answer, either on your own or together with your significant other, to better determine what ground rules will work best for your relationship. Like all the questions in this book, they'll be numbered by chapter, so you can write in your workbook or list your answers in a personal journal. Choose whichever works best for you, and allows you to provide detailed, thoughtful responses.

1.1 - Have you participated in cognitive behavioral therapy before, with a professional?

1.2 - If so, do you remember it as a positive or negative experience?

1.3   - What were some of the best things you learned from it?

1.4   - What do you wish had been handled differently?

1.5   - Close your eyes, and envision yourself walking past a group of people in a discussion. Imagine three things that would encourage you to join their conversation--this can be anything from the group's physical appearance, sound, smell, or subject matter. What are three things that would make you feel welcome, intrigued, and comfortable joining in?

1.6   - Again, close your eyes, and envision the same circumstance. What are three things that would encourage you to walk past this group without stopping?

1.7   - Would you consider yourself a morning person, or an evening person? How much does your sleep schedule impact your ability to communicate effectively with friends, co-workers, or family?

1.8   - In the past, did your parents, teachers, bosses, or other authority figures call you by a different name when they gave you praise or criticism? Were there particular phrases you heard that

would alert you to the fact that a stern lecture or punishment was coming?

1.9   - In your memory, what was harder to handle: receiving a stern lecture from a parental figure one on one, behind closed doors, or being disciplined in school, or another public place, where others could see and hear the interaction?

1.10   – Can you think of any particular words which you are particularly sensitive to? Perhaps a term that is generally considered neutral, but stings like a slur when it's directed at you?

1.11 - Imagine you are in a store, trying to purchase an item that you aren't too familiar with--maybe a computer, or a new pair of jeans in a style you don't normally wear. You need assistance from a salesperson to figure out what to buy. What could a salesperson do to help you feel confident in your purchase?

1.12 - What behaviors might discourage you from trusting their recommendations?

1.13 - How does it make you feel if the salesperson is distracted by their phone, or sharing a private laugh with a co-worker?

1.14 - What, if anything, would be a deal-breaker for you, inspiring you to walk out of the store, or write a negative review of your experience online?

1.15 - What, if anything, would inspire you to tell their supervisor that the salesperson did a great job and made you feel valued as a customer?

1.16 - Now let's reverse the roles. Imagine yourself working (in any environment). Today, someone with the power to make or break your paycheck wants your help with an important project. What could they do to help you feel confident in assisting them?

1.17 - What might they do that would lead you to feel nervous or inadequate?

1.18 - Is there anything they could do that would be a deal- breaker, inspiring you to refuse the project or quit the job?

1.19 - What could they do to help you feel enthusiastic about assisting them again in the future?

Have these questions given you any insight into your particular communication style? You might use them to create some additional rules that are specific to your personalities. For example, your partner may not feel capable of adhering to these ground rules when they are sleep deprived, while you may have horrible memories associated with public humiliation. In this case, you could add two additional ground rules: for one, no important discussions or arguments after ten o'clock at night, and for another, no tense conversations in public places.

After reviewing these guidelines and questions, you and your partner can write out a list of communication rules which you've agreed upon. You may find it particularly useful to keep this list physically accessible during intense discussions or arguments. A piece of

paper is no match for a counselor or mediator, but it can help to fill the same role, releasing either partner from the responsibility of being the communication watchdog. If ground rules are broken or bent, don't let yourself get riled in pointing out the demerits of your partner's behavior; the list of rules is unbiased, so let it play the role of referee.

Armed with this list, you can discuss almost any subject productively and respectfully. But how can you initiate the conversation you want to have? The next chapter will deal with setting the tone of your interactions and managing expectations, so read on to prepare yourself for even more successful communication.

Chapter 2

Setting the Mood

Picture this: you've just been offered an amazing job or promotion. You'd previously considered taking your relationship to the next level (moving in, marriage, children, a big move, whatever this may mean for you) but with this new position, you suddenly feel the time is right to move forward and hit the ground running.

You float through your day, whistling and grinning. You can't wait to tell your partner the good news. At the end of the workday, you stop to pick up something special for your partner--flowers, dinner, maybe something nice to drink, or a gift you've had your eye on--to make the evening memorable; then you head home, a bit nervous, but excited.

Then you come through the door, and before you get the chance to explain, you can immediately see that your partner is peeved.

"You're late," they say, arms crossed. "You promised you'd call if you were going to be late."

You did make this promise, but in all the excitement of the day, you forgot.

"I'm sorry," you start to say, but your partner doesn't want to listen to your apology.

"I made dinner, and it's cold now! I'm sick of this. I feel like I can't count on you, you never stay true to your word…"

Now how do you feel? Still excited to take the next step together?

We've all had moments when our greatest expectations were met with miserable realities. There's nothing more disappointing than seeing our best-laid plans blow up in our faces, especially when those plans involve the people we love.

Imagine that you could go back in time and change some circumstances that led up to this fight. What would you do differently, if you knew your partner would be so dismayed by your late arrival? If you knew they had made dinner for you? How might your partner have reacted differently, if they knew the reason for your lateness beforehand?

Managing expectations is an important part of any relationship and a fundamental aspect of boundary work. It's a practice that, when used frequently, can prevent these types of miscommunications before they even occur, or at least help to minimize feelings of confusion, discord, and unreliability in your relationship.

The first step is to take full ownership of your own expectations. Often, when you feel an intimate and deep connection with another person, it's too easy to forget that no one, no matter how much they love you, can read your mind. Your partner can't be held accountable for knowing what you want if you don't express your desires clearly. When expectations are presumed rather than communicated, you and your partner will regularly find yourselves on completely different pages, frequently disappointed by problems that would have had easy solutions in the past, but are now quite complicated to untangle.

Expectation management isn't only a valuable tool for preventing or de-escalating the conflict. It can be useful in all your day-to-day interactions, with friends, colleagues, family, and of course your partner. Most of us already incorporate this practice subconsciously whenever we make plans with others. If you agree to meet a friend at a restaurant for dinner, but get stuck in traffic on the way there, sending them a message to warn them you'll be late is a simple, easy way to manage your friend's expectations and set yourself up for an enjoyable evening. Likewise, you might plan to host a party

and send out invitations that mention a dress code, helping to prepare your guests for the atmosphere they'll find when they arrive. Lots of us manage expectations every day without even realizing we do it; we start a conversation with a smile to assure people we'll be safe and pleasant to talk to, or we wear headphones in public when we'd prefer not to be bothered. Some of us even choose our clothes and grooming styles as a way to manage other people's expectations of our personalities.

Do your best to become more conscious of the ways you do (or don't) manage expectations with your partner.

As often as possible, make an effort to prepare them, verbally or with nonverbal cues, for the next steps of the journey you take together. As an example, if you're considering inviting your partner to move in with you, a first step might be to clear out a sock drawer and offer it up for them to use. Alternatively, you might gradually increase the amount of time spent together during the week and start a conversation about sharing household responsibilities before extending an official invitation. On the other hand, these gestures would be confusing and misleading if you're not at all interested in sharing your living space. It's important to be as honest with your partner and with yourself; if you've been dissatisfied in the relationship lately, it doesn't help anyone to pretend that everything is hunky dory, or that you're ready for commitment when you truly are not.

Managing your partner's expectations is about regulating what you promise on your end--it's not about managing or manipulating your partner's behavior. Here's a common example of this misconception: a person might need to have a tough discussion with their loved one, and anticipate a volatile response. To manage the situation, they could choose to broach the subject in a public place, like a nice restaurant, hoping to discourage their partner from making a scene.

While this impulse is understandable--many of us are afraid of confrontation, after all--it is an example of shame-based manipulation, a tactic that should never be used with someone you care about.

By contrast, managing expectations means preparing your partner for what's coming in a way that displays empathy; you might tell your partner that you'd like to talk about something and make arrangements to meet someplace where you'll have privacy and where you'll both feel comfortable expressing yourselves.

If you've been feeling disconnected, growing apart or fighting more than you'd like, manage expectations of the future by making it clear to your partner that you want to work together to repair and improve the relationship. This might be awkward or uncomfortable to say plainly and out of the blue. In that case, there are plenty of ways you can show your partner rather than telling them. Make more eye contact and smile at them--facial expressions do an enormous amount of communication work for us when we can't find the right words, so try to be conscious of what your expressions are saying. Reach out to hold their hand, especially if you want to reassure them of your commitment to moving forward.

If you know your partner is comfortable with public displays of affection, make your adoration obvious in front of mutual friends and acquaintances; this will show your partner that you're proud to be with them and help to manage their expectation of your commitment to the relationship.

Let's use this workbook as a concrete example. Ideally, you'll want to use it with your significant other, but there are plenty of different ways it can be used. So, to get the most out of it, the first thing you'll want to do is identify your own expectations of the experience. Close your eyes, take a deep breath, and think about your expectations. Are they realistic? Of course, you're only on the second chapter, so it's hard to know what to expect exactly, but most of us can feel it in our guts when we're expecting too much out of any situation. This book is a useful tool, but it isn't magic. Will it single-handedly solve every problem in your relationship and personal life, and lead you swiftly to a future of pure unadulterated bliss, all without ever asking you to lift a finger? Probably not. Will this book be able to fix a relationship between two people who really aren't good for each other? Doubtful.

When you close your eyes and really check in with your desires, you might sometimes find they're a bit over the top or out of reach. That's okay and common, but do your best to let go of unrealistic expectations.

If you can't let go of them entirely, then think about how you might translate these inaccessible wishes into more reasonable goals. Could you read this book on your own to gain some new perspective on yourself and the role you play in your relationship? Absolutely. Could you use it with your partner to build a stronger connection, or start to repair a fracture in the relationship? Certainly. Could you keep it handy and read a chapter or two anytime you feel like your relationship could use some renewed excitement? Without a doubt.

Really listen to your heart here, and try to understand what it wants to get out of this experience. You probably wouldn't have made this purchase if you didn't want to get something out of it, whether that's entertainment, advice on a confusing issue, a guide to communicating about something that's been bothering you, or a pathway to deeper intimacy. All of these things are possible, but knowing what you want is the best way to ensure you're setting the mood and managing your partner's expectations as you strive to reach that goal. If you want to work through book activities together, you'll need to make sure your partner is on board. How can you bring a workbook like this to the table and encourage enthusiasm from your partner? How can you make them feel most at ease?

Whatever tactic you use, it's best to focus on optimism when asking your partner to work on your relationship. Highlight the positive things you hope to get out of these activities, rather than to dwell on the negative aspects of your relationship that might need work.

Some chapters will feature subjects that are more difficult than others, touching on personal issues and other matters of great sensitivity. To set yourself and your partner up for success, it might be best to review each chapter or activity before diving into it. If you've set the mood with candlelight and sultry music, you'll both be disappointed to take a quiz about your parents.

Get into the practice of checking in, asking your partner if they are comfortable discussing any topic before you start throwing questions at them. Be willing to put the topic aside if your partner isn't ready for it or comfortable with it. Conversely, you can warn your partner that certain subjects will be challenging for you to discuss, even if you are willing to try. In this way, managing expectations can be a lot like giving directions from the passenger seat of a car; sometimes, telling your partner to go left just a few seconds before the turn comes up can make a world of difference to your enjoyment of the ride.

If you'd prefer to work through the book on your own first, there's no need to check in with your partner every step of the way--in fact, you don't even have to tell them this book exists, if you feel at all self- conscious about your reading material. Still, you may want at least to let your partner know that you've been doing some pointed reflection on your relationship. Otherwise, sudden changes in your behavior may strike your partner as erratic, confusing, or insincere.

Never underestimate the impact of mood lighting, good music, or aromatherapy. If you need to start an intense conversation with your partner--whether it's a positive or negative topic--things will go much more smoothly if you can help your partner to feel eased into it. This is why the concept of small-talk exists; if deep conversations are like lake water, then small talk is the way that we dip our toes in before making a cannonball dive. The tempo of your interaction can also have an enormous impact on the outcome. Imagine you dipped your toe in the water, and your partner grabbed your hand to pull you in before you had the chance to decide how you felt about the temperature? Or, say you dipped your toes in at noon and found the water temperature to be perfect—would you still be ready to jump in at midnight based on that evaluation?

Finally, it's always best to start intense discussions from a place of calm, so learn to recognize symptoms of stress in yourself and your partner, and find strategies to promote quick relaxation (breathing exercises, for example, can be amazingly helpful). If you can't find a place of calm, or land on the same page as your partner to begin, the conversation may need to wait for a more appropriate time.

Chapter 3

The "Obvious" Questions

We have plenty of strategies now for having tense conversations. But relationships aren't ultimately about managing conflict; they're about having fun and feeling connected!

So, let's get the ball rolling with an easy game. This list of "ultimates" may seem fairly basic, but sometimes when you fall for someone, you're too overwhelmed with emotion to stop and ask what your partner's favorite book is. It's never a bad time to check in and see how well you really know your partner's likes, dislikes, and background.

Read the list aloud for each other, one at a time. State your answers aloud or jot them down on paper. Either way, try to answer these prompts in ten seconds or less--don't overthink your responses, just go with your gut. Use a timer or let your partner count down from ten to keep this activity quick and exciting.

Alternatively, if you and your partner have been involved for a long time, try answering the prompts on your partner's behalf, and then have them grade your accuracy--but remember not to be disappointed by incorrect answers! These are simply opportunities to learn something new and forge a deeper connection.

The "Ultimates" List

Got your timer ready? Alright, name your...

3.1   - Favorite fruit

3.2   - Favorite color

3.3   - Favorite band or artist

3.4   - Oldest friend

3.5   - Favorite movie

3.6   - Favorite book

3.7   - Most valued possession

3.8   - Favorite sport

3.9   - Favorite store

3.10 - First job

3.11 - Closest friend

3.12 - Favorite season

3.13 - Favorite song

3.14 - Favorite tech toy

3.15 - Biggest pet peeve

3.16 - Favorite dessert

3.17 - Least favorite food

3.18   - Greatest fear

3.19   - Strangest family member

3.20   - Favorite hobby

3.21   - Longest relationship before this

3.22   - Favorite curse word

3.23   - Worst habit

3.24   - Dream job

3.25   – All-time favorite activity

How did that go? Did you learn anything about your partner that surprised you?

Perceptions: How We See Ourselves and Each Other

No matter how long you've been together, remembering the reasons why you first fell for each other can always help to bring you and your partner closer together. It's exhilarating to get a taste of how others perceive you because it involves a hint of risk--they may see something in you that you consider unappealing, after all, or notice something about which you are self-conscious. But if you can trust that your partner will be sensitive in performing this exercise, you're likely to walk away from it with a new source of self-esteem, and a refreshed sense of excitement for your relationship, as well.

It's important to be sensitive as you discuss physical appearance with your partner. You want to feel safe in being honest with one another to keep communication lines open. Don't ruin your chances by mocking your partner, poking fun at their insecurities, or dismissing their concerns.

You may find it helpful to connect while discussing these questions physically. Hold hands, play footsie, or lean on each other throughout this or any other conversation in which one or both people are likely to feel vulnerable. It will help you both to feel safe and trustful.

You can also do the first piece of this exercise on your own if you feel bashful or find it difficult to talk about yourself. Write your responses down, though, and keep them in mind as you move through the following activities.

Describing Yourself

3.26 - When you look in the mirror today, what do you like most about yourself?

3.27 - What bothers you the most?

3.28 - Is there anything you think about changing?

3.29 - When you think of your adolescent self in comparison to your present-day self, what changes are you most proud of?

3.30 - Is there anything you miss about the younger version of you?

3.31 - Which is your favorite of your features? (hair, eyes, mouth, skin, etc.)

3.32 - Which is your least favorite, or the feature about which you feel most insecure?

3.33 - Would you say you take pride in your appearance? Or do you tend to value function over fashion, or convenience over personal expression?

3.34 - How would you describe the sound of your voice?

3.35 - How would you describe your skin?

3.36 - How would you describe your figure and stature?

3.37 - How would you describe your style? Use three words or less.

3.38 - Do you consider yourself old-fashioned, or cutting edge?

3.39 - Would you describe yourself as tough, or soft? (remember there are no wrong answers here--you can interpret this literally, figuratively, or both)

3.40 - If you had an aura, what color would it be?

3.41 - What animal best represents you?

What Your Partner Sees in You

Now that you've done some reflection on how you each view yourselves, let's ask some questions to figure out how you view each other. The answers you find might surprise you. Perhaps you've confessed that you don't like your nose, but what if that's your partner's favorite one of your features? Maybe you think your aura is orange, but they see it as purple.

Try not to judge your partner's responses to any of these questions. If you feel a visceral need to react, take a few deep breaths before you say anything, and choose your words wisely. You want your partner to trust you, and feel that anytime you choose to work on your relationship together, you've created a safe emotional space. Especially if your partner is sensitive to criticism, judgmental reactions can shut down communication in a lasting way.

Say your partner's answers are stoic and short; you've described every line and curve of their face, the precise shade of their hair and eye color, their height, weight, figure and style, and all they can say about you is that you're "cute." You could roll your eyes, sigh, cross your arms and become defensive; you could choose to be offended, and tell them immediately how bothered you are by their lack of willingness to expand on the subject.

But if you want your partner to feel comfortable opening up to you, being honest and expressing their vulnerable side--which is quite difficult for a lot of people--then the best way to react is with patience.

Calmly explain to your partner what you wish for, and why. "I'd love to hear more of your thoughts," you might say, "and since I've shared so much with you, I feel hurt when your responses are short and lack detailed thought." Again, avoid making assumptions about what your partner thinks, feels, or knows. Asking for clarification and declaring your desires can always improve your communication.

3.42 - How would you describe my looks to someone in your life who's never met me?

3.43 - How would you describe my personality to them?

3.44 - List three things about me that you find particularly attractive. Note: these do not have to be physical traits!

3.45 - Do I remind you of anyone in particular?

3.46 - Close your eyes and think of me. Do I have a scent?

3.47 -What color do you think is most flattering on me?

3.48 - Are there particular activities during which you find you are especially attracted to me? (For example: I am most attracted to you when you are laughing; I love to watch you play guitar; I think you really shine when you're leading a team at work; It's amazing to see how much you light up when you're with your children, and so on.)

3.49 - Do you remember our first encounter or the first time you noticed me?

3.50 - What about me stands out most in this memory?

3.51 - Is there anything you've discovered about me in our time together that's particularly surprised you or subverted your expectations? If so, what?

3.52 – Would you describe me as tough, or soft?

3.53 – Would you say I am old-fashioned, or cutting edge?

3.54 – If I had an aura, what color would it be?

3.55 – What animal best represents me, in your opinion?

3.56 – How would you describe my style in three words or less?

3.57 – How much time would you guess I spend on my appearance each week?

3.58 – Would you describe me as young-at-heart, or as an old soul?

3.59 – Which of my features is your favorite?

3.60 – Say you're a candid photographer, and you want to show me a photo that

captures the way you see me. What does this photo look like? Use as much detail as you can here.

Comparing and Contrasting Perceptions of Shared Experience

To end this chapter, here's another quick exercise to help remind you that you and your partner experience the world differently. This is important to remember whenever conflicts or miscommunications come up;

check in with reality, and with each other, to make sure you're not just arguing two different sides of the same coin.

You'll want to have a timer handy, as well as paper and writing utensils. Find an art book in a store, or simply go online to look up a painting. It can be almost any painting you want to choose, just make sure it's one with a lot of details. Most works by Salvador Dali, Vincent Van Gogh or Hieronymus Bosch will suit this activity well.

Using your timer, examine the painting for one full minute with your partner, trying to take in as many details as possible.

When the minute is over, look away from the painting. Get your pens and paper, and reset your timer for five minutes. Now, with each of you working on your own, write down as many details as you can remember from the painting--specific colors, number of flower petals, characters, symbols, buildings, anything. Write this information as a list.

When five minutes is up, consult the painting again and go over your lists together. If you're the type who needs to keep score in order to enjoy a game, then mark any item you both noted with a heart, and mark any differences with stars.

What does that mean? Honestly, it can mean whatever you want it to because neither a heart nor a star is a bad thing in this scenario! If you and your partner have similar perspectives on some things, that's fantastic-- but differing views can be great as well, so long as

you respect each other and value the strength that can be found in your differences.

Keep the results of this exercise in mind the next time you and your partner disagree about your memories of a shared experience; even when you see things entirely differently, there's still a chance that you're both right. You may simply be seeing two different halves of the same whole truth.

Chapter 4

The "Little" Questions

Before we dive into this chapter, let's start with a couple of quick questions. Jot your answers down if you like, or simply keep them in mind as you read on.

Ready? Alright, here we go.

First: what is the most thoughtful gift you've ever received? Not just the most elaborate or expensive-- we're looking for the most considerate, heartwarming gesture that's ever been made for your benefit. This might not be a physical object, and it may not have cost a single dollar.

What made this gift especially thoughtful or valuable to you?

Second: what is the most disappointingly impersonal gift you've ever received? Again, your answer doesn't necessarily need to be based on monetary value, or the degree of effort made to secure the gift.

Why do you think you were disappointed by this gift?

Any occasion that calls for an exchange of gifts can be extremely stressful. You scramble around in search of a perfect present to give your significant other--something that you know they want, though they haven't explicitly told you so, or as the old adage advises, something that's perfect for them, but which they would never buy for themselves. That's a fairly tall order, isn't it? When you really think about it, though, it's absurd to worry that any gift you give won't be good enough to warrant gratitude and appreciation. It's a gift after all--you're spending your own time, money, or energy to give your partner something for free when the alternative is for them to receive nothing. Shouldn't we always be grateful--no, thrilled--to receive any

kind of gift at all? And in turn, shouldn't we always feel confident in giving them?

If you and your partner have done the work of managing expectations for yourselves and each other in a productive way, you shouldn't have to worry that your gift will fail to meet their standards of monetary cost or effort.

But if this is the case, and you still feel that twinge of self-doubt and anxiety in your gut while gift-shopping, probably it's because you've internalized the notion that gifts are a form of non-verbal communication. We learn this when we are children with no money to spend on gifts for our parents and friends, and we are told instead to make them cards, or crafts that consist primarily of popsicle sticks and glitter. We are told that it's perfectly fine to give a gift that has no obvious function or relevance and that it doesn't matter if the gift is given late because it's the thought behind it that counts.

Most of us are taught that the purpose of gifts is to show people how much they mean to us through our generosity. So it's no small wonder that many of us have developed anxiety about gift-giving in adulthood; we worry, whether consciously or subconsciously, that the strength or validity of our love will be judged and evaluated based on the quality of the gift. Unfortunately, quality is subjective, so what chance do you really have of hitting this moving target?

Let's think back to the answers we gave at the start of this chapter. When you think of the gift that most disappointed you, ask yourself: was this really an objectively bad present? Or might it have been a perfect gift for someone--just not for me?

When you think of the most thoughtful gift you received, ask yourself: did I appreciate this because of its price tag, or its novelty? Or did it mean so much because it came from someone I care about and showed me that they really understand who I am?

Generally, anything that is shiny or new can make a good gift. But a gesture that is personalized, and speaks to the recipient's unique set of preferences and needs? That's something much more meaningful. Now, bring that thoughtful, personalized gift to mind again. What if your partner could recreate a smaller version of this experience every month for you? Every week, or maybe even every day? Can you imagine how special and lucky you might feel? Wouldn't this help you to feel valued and well understood? Would you feel inspired to reciprocate?

Whenever you can show your partner that you understand and appreciate them, you're helping to inspire those very same feelings inside them. And it can be done without spending a dime, lifting a finger, or sprinkling glitter on a single popsicle stick. All that you need to do is pay close attention.

The Devil is in the Details

Do you consider yourself a detail-oriented person?

Whether you do or not, chances are you noticed lots of small details about your partner when you first met. In the early stages of a relationship, people are usually highly focused on getting to know one another, asking explicit questions, watching each other's facial expressions and body language for clues to what they might be thinking or feeling. Falling for someone new can often feel like an all-encompassing experience, because we are on high alert in this person's presence, wanting to absorb every look, touch, or sound that they make. Or, perhaps you met your significant other after encountering major challenges in previous relationships; you might have paid close attention to the details of your partner's appearance, speech, and behavior at first, all because you were looking out for warning signs of trouble.

Either way, most of us are in the habit of doing a little detective work whenever we forge a new connection, learning as much as we can about a person's behaviors and background, likes and dislikes.

As time goes on and you grow more comfortable in the relationship, you may start to feel complacent, falling into the habit of making assumptions about your partner and paying less attention to their nonverbal cues.

This is often a precursor to a slump--a period of apathy and decreased emotional or physical intimacy that is often mistaken by serial monogamists for a sign that the relationship is doomed to failure. Realistically, though, a sudden loss of enthusiasm or connection that comes 6-9 months after the start of a new relationship (or 6-9 months after moving in together, 6-9 months after getting married, 6-9 months after retiring together, whatever the changing circumstance may be) is most likely a sign that one or both parties have gotten lazy about maintaining the curiosity they

exhibited early on. Sparks can almost always be reignited, but only if both parties are willing to devote energy to relationship work.

"Relationship work?" you might be saying right now, recoiling from this book in horror. "I thought relationships were supposed to be about love and trust, comfort and fun--not work!"

Sorry to be the bearer of disappointing news, but every relationship-- romantic, platonic or familial--is like a newborn infant with an invisible body. Even if you can't see it or hear it crying, it needs to be nurtured and cared for; it needs to be taught basic skills in its early formative stages; it needs to be fed well in order to grow strong; it needs to be regularly cleaned up and groomed to stay healthy; and above all, it needs regular maintenance, care, and attention. Like a growing child, it doesn't need these things constantly--when circumstances allow, it's perfectly reasonable to leave a child sleeping or playing on their own for a short while so that you can focus on your own needs. But a child is never done needing attention; they will never reach a critical mass, a point at which they have received enough care and no longer need any maintenance. Your relationship is the same way. Over time, it can grow strong enough to withstand difficulties or short droughts of attention, but it will never become self-sustaining or invulnerable. It will always require effort on your part.

Just as it is easier to wash your dishes daily, rather than to let them stack up for weeks before washing, your relationship work will be a lot less daunting if you keep at it consistently. It will be easier to keep a spark alive than to reignite one that has already fizzled long ago. In this chapter, we'll focus on questions and behaviors that will help you to do just that. You'll want to keep playing detective with your partner, regardless of how well you think you already know them, taking note of the little things in the same way that you might if you were writing a biography about them. The goal here is not only to display your curiosity to your partner (although reminding someone that you find them interesting can go a long way towards rekindling a dying flame) but also to find ways to show your partner that you're still paying close attention and learning from these little details.

The "Little" Questions — Preferences and Personality

Interview each other as though you are writing a story about your significant other for a local newspaper. Write your partner's answers down and keep them for yourself; these may come in handy the next time you are brainstorming a gift or loving gesture.

4.1 - Are you early, right on time, or fashionably late?

4.2 - Would you rather be hot, or cold?

4.3 - Saturday night with ten acquaintances, or Sunday morning with one close friend?

4.4 - Do you consider yourself a morning or evening person?

4.5 - Do you prefer background noise, or quiet?

4.6 - Do you consider yourself an introvert or extrovert?

4.7 - Do you have a favorite newspaper, blog, or other periodicals?

4.8 - Would you rather work with your hands or your head?

4.9 - Say you've become a high school teacher. Would you teach Math or English?

4.10 - Drama or physical education?

4.11 - History, or science?

4.12 - If there were a fire in your home and you had time to grab only one item, what would it be?

4.13 - If someone made a movie of your life, what would it be named? And what genre would it be?

4.14 - What type of music would be used for the soundtrack?

4.15 - If you could sit down for a night of dinner and drinks with anyone, living or dead, who would it be?

4.16 - What would you ask them?

4.17 - Is there any book or movie that you don't think you could ever get tired of?

4.18 - If you could be granted the power of clairvoyance or telekinesis, which would you choose?

4.19 - Why? And what would you do with the power?

4.20 - Do you have any recurring nightmares? If so, what are they?

4.21 – Do you prefer minimalist décor, or eclectic?

4.22 – If you could either fly or breathe underwater, which ability would you choose?

4.23 – In tough decisions, do you follow your head or your heart?

4.24 – If you could be either entirely invisible or so famous that you'd need a bodyguard to leave your house, which would you choose?

4.25 – Which would you prefer to retain in your old age: your mind, or your body?

Sometimes, couples encounter major challenges that truly overshadow their ability to enjoy each other's company--differing views on moral values, or disparate plans for the future--but more often than not, what makes or breaks a couple is the small stuff. The boring, day-to-day, minor details that add up to your overall impressions of one another will have a much greater effect on your happiness than the big celebrations or major catastrophes. If you think of your relationship as a castle you're building together, the big moments in life are like rough cut boulders, and the little details are like bricks. When a storm comes, a castle built of many small, cleanly cut and well-placed bricks will stand stronger in its foundation than a large haphazard pile of rocks, won't it?

One easy way to strengthen your connection is to focus on building that castle, brick by brick, with small thoughtful gestures. Learn as much as you can about your partner's experiential preferences: what amuses them, what makes them feel comfortable and safe and loved. Then, try to bring more of these things into the time you share together. Think of these as opportunities to give small, thoughtful gifts, as we defined them earlier in the chapter. They can be immaterial and inexpensive, so long as these gestures include a personal touch. By contrast, a bouquet of red roses is a costly and impressive gift, but it is also a romantic cliché; your partner might appreciate the beauty of them, but they might also be left feeling like you're taking a paint-by-numbers approach to love. With your partner, aim to be specific rather than generic, and consistent rather than extravagant. Over time, a lot of small thoughtful moments will be more meaningful than one grand gesture.

Don't save this practice for special occasions--this exercise can be as simple, inexpensive and frequent as finding out exactly how your partner enjoys their morning coffee or tea and making it for them whenever you have the chance. You might try to incorporate their favorite color into your wardrobe more often or pick up their favorite treat from the grocery store without being asked to. If you learn that your partner has a stressful work meeting every day at mid-morning, you might adopt the habit of sending a message to check in most days at lunchtime. Exchanged gestures like this will help you to feel connected, supported, and valued regularly, building a strong foundation for a happy future together.

The more you learn about your partner, the easier it will be to find ways to brighten their day.

More "Little" Questions — Experience and Emotion

4.26 - What's your ideal way to wake up?

4.27 - What's your ideal way to fall asleep?

4.28 - What do you crave when you're feeling down: sweet, sour, spicy or savory treats?

4.29 - You have an hour to kill at home; would you play a game? Read a book? Exercise? Take a nap?

Something else?

4.30 - Say you wake up sick. What could I do to make you as comfortable as possible?

4.31 - What book or movie do you want?

4.32 - What kind of soup?

4.33 – Do you want to be alone? Or should I stay close by to help out?

4.34 - Let's say you've been a bystander to a traumatic event. You're home and safe now; what could I do to help you feel calm?

4.35 - We go to a restaurant, and you excuse yourself to use the washroom. The server comes by for our drink order. What beverage would you want me to get for you?

4.36 - Say you've hosted a party. At the end of the night, you find that some guests have made a mess in your bedroom, having lost an earring in your laundry bin and upending it on the floor to find it. There is also a pile of dirty dishes in the kitchen sink. Which mess do you tackle first? Do you clean up as soon as your guests depart, or let it wait till the morning?

4.37 - What's your favorite part of a typical day?

4.38 - What part of your day do you dread most?

4.39 - Can you enjoy things (like movies, books, games, etc.) repeatedly? Or is novelty more enjoyable for you?

4.40 - Do you like surprises? Or do you tend to get anxious without a plan?

4.41 - Say you wake up one morning, suddenly immortal and invincible. What's the first thing you would do?

4.42 – What does a bad day at work entail for you? What makes it so unpleasant?

4.43 – You just won a promotion (or another coveted prize)—how would you like to celebrate?

4.44 – If you could instantly change three circumstances in your life with just a snap of your fingers, what would you change?

4.45 – Imagine a picture perfect day. What does that look like for you? What do you do? Where do you go? What do you eat and drink? Who's there with you? Use as much detail as you can here.

Chapter 5

The "Big Picture" Questions

When you were a young child, how did you picture your future? Did you have concrete plans for a sensible career, like becoming a doctor and opening a family practice? Maybe, but chances are you imagined your future circumstances to be a bit more extraordinary. You might have wanted to become an astronaut or an explorer, a movie star or a pop music sensation, a president or international spy.

It's natural for children to think of themselves as special, destined for greatness. Other children your age probably wouldn't blink at your declared intention to become a famous professional athlete and go to the Olympics one day. Only adults would express doubt in your dreams because only they would be aware of how steeply the odds are stacked against you. Do you remember the first time someone reacted to your sky-high ambitions with skepticism?

It can be heartbreaking to see someone laugh at your dreams, no matter how far out of reach they are, especially if the person laughing is someone you love. Most of us learn at some point in childhood to filter ourselves in social situations, never bragging about our ambitions unless we are reasonably certain of our competence and ability to achieve these goals. But when you meet someone special and begin to trust them, you start to let your guard down. You allow yourself to feel vulnerable around them. This is why some people say that falling in love can make the old feel young again; when we strive for emotional intimacy, we often expose a childlike side of our personalities that no one else but our partner gets to see. We express hopes and dreams to them that we might feel too self- conscious to admit to anyone else.

Lots of us harbor bigger-than-life hopes for our futures, even if we realize these dreams are unrealistic. It's hard to pull ourselves through the boring and difficult times if we don't feel that we're working towards something better, like a light at the end of a tunnel. Some of us may be embarrassed to share these hopes and dreams with anyone, even those we feel closest with. But an important step in growing closer is learning to trust your partner with the most vulnerable parts of yourself, even those wishes and desires that might seem childlike or naive.

Allow yourself to share your starry-eyed inner child with your partner, and encourage them to do the same with you. Seeing this side of each other will help to bring you closer together.

Furthermore, as you grow older, you may come to find that some dreams which once seemed impossible to achieve are actually well within your reach. It's always a good idea to get to know what your partner's vision of personal success and fulfillment looks like, because you may find yourself at their side when this vision becomes a reality.

Miracle Questions

We call these "miracle questions" because they aren't meant to be grounded in your reality. While you go through them, imagine that any roadblocks which might stand between you and your dreams have magically evaporated. Unlike the last chapter, this questionnaire isn't meant to guide you to a perfect gift or gesture. The point is to build deeper trust and connection with your partner, as well as to foster a sense of positivity and optimism in the relationship.

5.1 - You get a miraculous windfall--a raise, inheritance, or tax refund-- and you don't need to use it to pay bills. Do you spend it on vacation, or another type of splurge? Or do you invest or save it?

5.2 - Say you do go on a vacation. What country will you visit?

5.3 - Will you plan out your itinerary ahead of time? Or ask the locals for recommendations and play it by ear?

5.4 - Your job grants you a promotion to a position with two available locations: one is metropolitan, while the other is rural. Which would you choose and why?

5.5 - It's time for us to adopt a pet together. Is it a dog? Cat? Lion? Elephant? Another animal?

5.6 - You have the funds and the talent to design a home and have it built from the ground up. What does it look like?

5.7 - Where is it?

5.8 - How many rooms are there, and what is each used for? Give this some real consideration.

5.9 - By the time you've reached retirement age, how large of a family do you imagine you'll have?

5.10 - Imagine you've grown so successful at work that you can now set your own schedule. How would you design it? How many days off per week?

5.11 - How many vacation weeks per year?

5.12 - Would you work in the mornings or in the evenings?

5.13 - Would you work from home, or in an office?

5.14 - You're at the top of your field, and have a milestone birthday coming up. Your colleagues and loved ones throw an event in your honor. What does that look like to you? Is it a party? An awards ceremony? A roast? Formal or casual? Local, or a destination event? All day long, or all night long? Inside or outdoors?

5.15 - Say there is a natural disaster, and we are suddenly uprooted, displaced, and disengaged from our careers. Money is not an issue. What would you choose to focus your attention on, under these circumstances?

5.16 – If you could retire tomorrow, and spend the rest of your life focused on a leisure activity or hobby, what would it be?

5.17 – If you were elected president, what would be your first act after taking office?

5.18 – As president, what would you hope that your legacy would be?

5.19 - If you could explore outer space, or the uncharted depths of the ocean, which would you choose and why?

5.20 - Have you given any thought to the way you'd like your life to be celebrated after you're gone? If it's not too uncomfortable to think about, share your thoughts on this.

While answering these questions, you may start to notice trends in your partner's responses. Perhaps your partner's dreams for the future seem much further out of reach than yours; or maybe your partner doesn't appear, to you, to be working towards these goals at all. Try not to let this concern you too much. These questions are meant to give you a general sense of where your desires and values may lead you--they aren't meant to be a roadmap.

Ranking Priorities

This next exercise is meant to help you get a sense of where your partner's (or your own) values lie. There is often a vast difference between what we claim is most important to us, and what we pay the most attention to in reality. Societal pressures may persuade you to declare that you aim to be a devoted spouse, an attentive parent, a rising star in your career field, an easy-going friend, and a fitness guru, all while still attending faith-based services every weekend and starting up a charitable organization of your own. But there are only so many hours in a day, and only so much of you to go around. Ranking your priorities--even theoretical ones--can help you to understand what you and your partner truly desire most: what you care about enough to make time for it.

The lists below are activities or values that come in groups of five. Within the groupings, assign each to a number from one to five, with one being the activity you would choose to complete first. Assume that whatever task is assigned to number four will end up being rushed or haphazard, and number five isn't likely to get done at all.

5.21 - On vacation:

Visit art museums

Go for a hike in nature

Enjoy a three-course prix-fixe meal at a famous restaurant Ride over the city in a hot air balloon

Massages, mud baths and more at the spa

5.22 - For the weekend:

Brunch with friends Clubbing or partying

Laundry and other necessary chores

Faith services (or non-denominational weekly meeting) Relaxing on the couch

5.23 - In the morning before work:

Coffee or tea with a freshly cooked breakfast A good half hour of exercise

Pick an outfit and ensure you are groomed to perfection

Read the newspaper and fill out a crossword or sudoku puzzle

5.24 - For your birthday:

A perfect gift (a physical item) A gathering with loved ones

Time off from work and household responsibilities, so you can relax

An adventure or big surprise (concert tickets, a trip, etc.) A quiet and romantic night at home, just the two of us

5.25 - For your future:

A highly successful career A busy family life

To travel and see a great deal of the world Spiritual or philosophical enlightenment

A simple, stable and comfortable home life

Values

This exercise is a bit more grounded in reality. Focus on your own truth as you reply, rather than providing the answers you believe you should give. While it may feel odd to admit that your family isn't a high priority for you, for instance, it will certainly become clear to your partner over time. Being honest about values can help you both to get closer to achieving your goals because you'll waste less of your time and energy on maintaining charades.

How important are these things to you on a scale from 1 to 10 (1 being not very important, 5 being neutral, 10 being extremely important)?

5.26 - Holiday celebrations

5.27 - Maintaining your current social circle

5.28 - Travel/adventurous experiences

5.29 - Leisure time

5.30 - Career

5.31 - Family

5.32 - Arts/culture

5.33 - Religion or spirituality

5.34 - Financial stability

5.35 - Spontaneity

5.36 - Sticking to an established plan

5.37 - Recognition or accolades

5.38 - Personal Privacy

When you compare and contrast this list with your partner, don't panic at the differences you see, even if they look extreme on paper. The important thing isn't that all your desires and preferences align-- it's that you respect your partner's values and work to compromise wherever necessary.

Still worried? Differences in our value structures can be challenging, certainly. But there are plenty of politicians, movie stars, and other celebrities with life partners who absolutely hate the spotlight. Differences like this can keep relationships exciting over long periods of time. Some people find that their partner's contrasting views help to balance them out, expand their perspectives, and push them towards personal growth.

Differences don't have to be damning, but they do have to be appreciated rather than resented. Show support for your partner's values, hopes, and dreams, even if they don't always overlap with yours. Remember that often, we edit our life plans as we go to make room for the things and people we fall in love with along the way.

Chapter 6

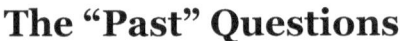

The "Past" Questions

As much as we like to wax poetic about living in the moment and leaving the past behind us, in reality, many of us carry our pasts around with us every day. The past can be a huge part of what informs our subconscious realities—and left unexamined, it can wreak havoc in our present-day relationships.

Your experiences in grade school, your first romantic relationship, your first job—these can all become ingrained in your psyche and impact your current attitudes about life. But if there's one single aspect of your past that you'll need to understand to break bad habits, escape vicious cycles, accomplish your goals and function healthily in your relationship, it's this: Who raised you?

Attachment Theory

There are many different schools of therapy, and not all of them see eye-to-eye; however, most of them agree that our early childhood experiences, as well as our extended relationships with parental figures, shape an enormous amount of our subconscious thought and behavior. Attachment theory is the idea that we are deeply attracted to relationship dynamics which remind us of our formative years—even if those dynamics are unhealthy for us.

It also suggests that most problems we express in relationships are a form of projection; in our partners, we seek out what we needed most from our parental figures but failed to receive.

Research in the field of psychology tells us that about half of all children are raised in an environment that teaches them secure attachment; these children get reliable love, support and attention from their caretakers, and as they grow, they are able to become independent, self-assured, reliable and trusting. Unfortunately, the other half of children are raised in environments that don't get it quite right. Children whose parents were not reliably supportive can develop an anxious attachment style, never able to trust that they can count on a partner, or that they are loved. Children whose parents were absent may grow up to use avoidant attachment as a coping skill, refusing to rely on others and developing a fear of physical or emotional closeness. Finally, some extremely unlucky children are raised in environments where they are simply exposed to too much abuse and trauma; these children will likely enact disorganized attachment behaviors in adulthood, which creates chaos and distrust in relationships.

Counselors often find it can be beneficial for struggling couples to learn about each other's childhood experiences because it can replace blame and confusion with sympathy and understanding. One may finally see that their partner's most frustrating or confounding habits are not meant to antagonize anyone--in fact, they may not be

conscious of the behavior at all, if it's something they learned early in life. Couples may discover that anger or resentment within their relationship is misdirected or misinformed.

Our experiences in the first few years of life leave lasting impressions on our psyches. These are the years during which the foundation of our attachment style is built, and it is also when we learn our primary coping mechanisms. Without some form of therapy or deep self-reflection, it is difficult to be fully conscious of how these experiences shape our adult personalities, but if you find you are experiencing repeated or cyclical issues in your relationships, it can be immensely helpful to explore these issues with a qualified therapist.

Your Childhood

Before beginning this questionnaire, it's presumed that you and your partner know some basics about each other's immediate families. If this isn't the case, it is recommended that you discuss who raised you, where you grew up, and whether or not you're still in touch with parental figures and siblings, before you start the exercise.

Please feel free to rephrase or tailor any of the below questions to reflect the specifics of your upbringing. Many people are raised by more or less than two parents, by parental figures of the same gender, and by individuals who do not share a romantic connection. Even so, these questions should be considered and answered thoughtfully. The specifics of the questions aren't important here--this exercise is simply an opportunity to reflect on the lessons you learned about interpersonal connections in early life, no matter who you learned those lessons from.

Remember to manage expectations here! Family history can be a challenging topic to discuss. You might want to take some steps to prepare yourselves first, and create a calm, safe space in which to talk. Light a candle, put on some soothing music, make some tea, or even trade neck massages to loosen yourselves up before you begin.

If you're still not comfortable discussing family history with your partner, now is the time to make that clear. You may find it easier to do so with the help of a therapist or counselor.

6.1 - What's your general impression of your childhood?

6.2 - Would you consider it a happy one?

6.3 - Can you remember a typical day of your life at the age of four or five?

6.4 - Where were you?

6.5 - Who was there?

6.6 - What kinds of things did you do?

6.7 - Do you have stronger memories of your mother figure or father figure? Or perhaps someone else who served as primary caregiver?

6.8 - How would you describe the relationship between your parental figures?

6.9 - How did they express affection to each other?

6.10 - How did they express frustration to one another?

6.11 - How did each of them express these emotions to you?

6.12 - How were these emotions expressed to your siblings, if you had any?

6.13 - Were displays of affection frequent, or infrequent?

6.14 - Were they verbal or physical? Neither, or both?

6.15 - How about expressions of anger, by comparison?

6.17 - Do you have any memories of specific conflicts that left a lasting mark on you? Maybe a conflict that confused you, or taught you an important lesson?

6.18 - What about expressions of love? Do any particular memories stand out in your mind?

6.19 - In what ways did your parents tell or show you that you were important to them?

6.20 - What about criticisms. How did your parents express them to each other, or to third parties?

6.21 - How were criticisms communicated to you?

6.22 - When difficulties arose, do you feel that your parents modeled healthy coping mechanisms for you?

6.23 - What about the way they handled stress did you admire?

6.24 - What do you hope to do differently?

6.25 - Were bedroom doors usually open or closed in your home?

6.26 - Was the front door or back door left unlocked?

6.27 - Were you often home alone and unsupervised?

6.28 - If you were usually supervised, how did you feel about your primary caretaker?

6.29 - Were rules in your home generally easy-going, or strict?

6.30 - How were disciplinary measures enforced?

6.31 - Did you have a relationship with your extended family? If so, what was it like?

6.32 - Did you feel secure as a child? Safe?

6.33 - If you had questions, concerns, or fears, who could you talk to about them?

6.34 - Do you remember the first time you went to a friend's home for dinner or a sleepover? Did you notice that your friend's family did things differently from your own?

6.35 - If so, what differences did you note? How did you feel about them?

6.36 - Did you stay in one place throughout your childhood, or move? If so, how often?

6.37 - How did you feel about the place you grew up in?

6.38 - If you were in one place throughout those developmental years, did you find it stimulating or boring?

6.39 - Did you feel accepted there?

6.40 - If you moved, did you find it difficult to adjust to change?

6.41 - How did moving impact your friendships and support system?

6.42 – What attitudes did your parental figures express about the move?

6.43 - Do you remember your earliest experiences with separation from a loved one or friend?

6.44 - Were you given guidance on how to handle it?

6.45 - What kinds of values did your parents purposefully teach you? This can encompass anything from traditional religious education to a parent teaching a child to value the arts through piano lessons.

6.46 - What lessons, if any, did your parents teach you without meaning to? As an example, a parent who never takes vacation might teach their child to equate professional success with self- worth without ever intending to. Likewise, a parent who is guarded or secretive may inadvertently teach their child to fear intimacy.

6.47 - When you envision your own future, does it look much like the household you grew up in?

6.48 - In what ways is it similar? How is it different?

If these questions proved difficult for you to answer or were painful to think about, don't beat yourself up over it--there is no reason to feel ashamed of your childhood experiences, no matter how "abnormal" they may seem to you. Remember, roughly half of all children are raised in an environment that teaches insecure attachment styles—it can't be abnormal if one out of every two people has a similar hurdle to overcome in relationships.

Still, knowing you're not alone may not be enough to keep negative or shameful thoughts at bay after all this reflection. You may have found that your own childhood involved a lot more neglect or trauma than you had previously realized, or your partner might have been the one to have this revelation. Maybe both of you have touched on some painful memories while reviewing this chapter, and you're now concerned about the compatibility of your respective attachment styles. In any of these circumstances, it's advisable that you explore the impact of your traumatic experiences with the guidance of a licensed professional, or the help of a support group.

It may be beneficial to do this outside of the context of your relationship-- meaning, if you see a counselor as a couple, it may still be wise to speak to a therapist one-on-one about your personal upbringing— especially if you struggle with any symptoms of codependency.

The legacy of childhood trauma doesn't heal on its own. If ignored, it won't dissipate over time, or evaporate due to distance. It can't be overcome with career success or high achievement, or even by love. Trauma that is left unexamined inside of us will come out in one way or another; usually, it rears its ugly head through our subconscious behaviors, creating roadblocks in our attempts to build healthy connections with others. It can be tempting to avoid addressing problems from the past, but if the health of this relationship is important to you, you'll be better off facing the past as soon as you are able.

Relationship History

It can be uncomfortable to discuss past romances with your current partner. Most people either speed through this conversation early in the relationship, avoid it entirely or tell a few white lies to make themselves look better and soothe their partners' fears. But relationships are where we learn communication skills in practice, so we do ourselves a disservice by sweeping past ones under the rug.

Imagine it's the end of your junior year in high school, and you have to transfer schools. How challenging would it be if your new school couldn't access any of your old records? How could you apply for higher education without transcripts? How would they know which classes to put you in without knowing what classes you've already taken?

Every relationship is different. There is no reason to fear that your partner will repeat negative behaviors with you just because they've had unhealthy relationships in the past. In fact, there's every chance that your partner learned from those negative experiences, and made a conscious choice to do things differently with you.

6.49 - Do you remember the first person you were romantically interested in?

6.50 - What attracted you to them?

6.51 - How would you describe your first relationship?

6.52 - How did you feel about yourself, within the context of this relationship?

6.53 - If you could travel back in time, and give your younger self advice on love and romance, what would it be?

6.54 - Are there any ideas about love and relationships that you once believed strongly, but no longer do?

6.55 - Any values you once held in a partner that is no longer important to you?

6.56 – What's the shortest relationship you've ever been in?

6.57 – What about the longest?

6.58 – Since you started dating, what's the longest period that you've remained single?

6.59 - Can you describe a moment from a past relationship wherein you felt really good about yourself? A moment when you felt loved, admired, valued, etc.?

6.60 - Can you share a memory from a past relationship wherein you felt your trust was betrayed? A moment wherein you felt taken for granted or undervalued?

6.61 - How did you handle it?

6.62 - How do you think you'd handle it if something similar happened again?

6.63 - Do you have any regrets about your past relationships? Anything you would do differently, given a chance?

6.64 - When your most recent relationship ended, do you feel you learned anything from it, in terms of what you do or do not want for our relationship?

6.65 – Which of your past relationships do you feel had the most impact on your outlook on love, and why?

If you or your partner are feeling tense after completing this exercise, shake out your hands and feet, take a few deep breaths to center yourselves, and go get some ice cream. Talk about something else for the rest of the day, something fun and light-hearted. Your past relationships shouldn't haunt you like ghosts, and you don't need to dwell on them or ruminate over what you could have done better. Consider only what you can learn from these experiences, and try to let the rest go.

Chapter 7

The "Future" Questions

If you're working through these chapters in order, you've already started thinking about the future. Chapter 5, in particular, may have helped you and your partner to start considering or discussing career goals, feelings about long term commitment, and the possibility of expanding your family--however, most of the questions in that chapter touched on these issues in an abstract, vague way. Here, we'll work on making more concrete plans for the future.

You'll want to really focus on answering the first set of questions for yourself, honoring your own personal truth, before tackling any further questions as a couple. In fact, you may find it helpful to complete the first set of questions alone, in privacy, at a point when you won't feel rushed to complete it.

You may also find that you're reluctant to share these answers with your partner right away; that's perfectly fine. For instance, if you realize throughout this questionnaire that becoming a parent is deeply important to you, but you know your partner has a lot of hesitation and fear centered around parenthood, there's no need to make a decision right now, one way or the other. You can decide to keep all these replies to yourself or to pick and choose which parts to share with one another.

The purpose of these questions is to refocus on managing your expectations for the future and try to get on the same page as your partner--this exercise is not designed to grade your personal competence or compatibility.

"Where are we headed as individuals? "

Pose this set of questions to yourself.

7.1   - How much thought have you given to your own future?

7.2   - Do you have specific or detailed plans for next year?

7.3   - The next five years?

7.4 - The next decade?

7.5 - Any plans that stretch even further into the future than a decade?

7.6 - Do you find you tend to think more in the long term or short term?

7.7 - Would you rather daydream about what you'll do this weekend, what you'll do next summer, or what you'll do five years from now?

7.8 - What do you imagine your next major purchase or financial investment will be? (Define the term "major" on a sliding scale here; either something worth a full month's salary or more or a larger purchase than you've made since you entered this relationship.)

7.9 – Do you feel that you're done with education? Or would you like to pursue it further?

7.10   - Do you have further ambitions for your career?

7.11   - If so, how close are you to realizing them?

7.12   - When it's time to settle down long-term, do you know where you'd like to live? This can be as specific as a particular city, or as vague as simply knowing what climate you like best, or knowing that you'd prefer not to settle down anywhere for too long until you are much older.

7.13   – Do you have the desire to become a parent? (Or if you are already, do you wish to parent more children?)

7.14   - Do you feel well-equipped to become a parent?

7.15 – Is there a specific age or deadline by which you expect to reach particular goals? (For example, you might plan to have your own business before you start a family, or to retire by the time your child graduates from college.)

7.16 - When you look forward to the future, are there any major circumstances in your life that you know will need to change for you to reach your goals? If so, what are they?

7.17 - Do you have a plan to change these circumstances?

7.18 - Do you have any major fears or anxieties about the future?

7.19 - If so, do you think you'd be comfortable discussing these anxieties with your partner, or someone else in your support system?

7.20 - Do you consider these fears and anxieties to be rational, irrational, or somewhere in between?

7.21 - Do you feel like you've changed or grown a lot within the past year?

7.22 - If so, how? And are you happy with the change?

7.23 - How do you think you might grow or change within the next five years?

7.24 - How do you feel about getting older? Do you look forward to it, or does the thought of aging cause you anxiety?

7.25 - What is one thing that you are worried you might not accomplish before your age disables you?

Whether or not you decide to share your answers with your partner,

it might be best to take some time to process these thoughts before moving through the next branch of this exercise. It's important to feel solid about your own future desires before you make any attempt to tailor them for your partner's sake.

"Where are we headed as a couple?"

This next set of questions concerns your future trajectory as a pair. Each is designed to facilitate a discussion that is more firmly grounded in reality than the conversations prompted in chapter 5, which featured a lot of speculative and abstract desires. You might want to think of the difference in these terms: if chapter 5 was about planning a dream vacation that you'd take someday in the hypothetical future with an unlimited budget, then by contrast, this chapter is asking you to plan an actual trip, this year, funded by the money you currently have in the bank.

Don't feel any pressure to get through all these questions in one session or even all in one week. Your collective future deserves deep thought and consideration.

If any of these questions expose a disparity, in terms of what you're each expecting from your future together, take some time to discuss the issue. How important is this goal to each of you, and how flexible can you be? Is this an instance wherein you might work together to design a compromise? Or could you each pursue your own separate goals without pulling too much energy or attention away from the relationship?

In these modern times, there are no road maps or blueprints to adhere to; prescribed gender roles and notions of what a typical couple should look like and how it should operate are changing every day. Don't be afraid to make outlandish suggestions for compromise, or to negotiate powerfully for your own needs in the relationship. Rather than worrying over how your relationship should progress, focus instead on how it does work now, and how it can work even better in the future to serve you both.

7.26 - How much thought have you given to our future together?

7.27 - In what ways do you feel that our goals are compatible?

7.28 - In what ways do you worry that our goals won't align in the years ahead?

7.29 - How do you feel about our current divisions of responsibility?

7.30 - Do you see any need for our respective roles in this relationship to change or evolve in the future?

If so, what changes would you want to see?

7.31 - When you envision the future, how much time do you think we'd spend together over a typical week?

7.32 - Do you know whether or not you'd like to be a primary caregiver to pets or children in the future?

7.33 - If you're not yet certain, are you comfortable discussing your hesitations and concerns with me?

(Keep this discussion vague and hypothetical, or skip it entirely for now, if the subject is especially sensitive for you. We'll touch on this issue more in the next chapter, and provide some additional tools for difficult discussions.)

7.34 - Do you think we've grown or changed as a couple over the past year?

7.35 - If so, how? And are you happy with the change?

7.36 - How much do you expect our relationship to grow or change in the coming year?

7.37 - How do you expect to handle unforeseen challenges to our plans?

7.38 - Can you list three goals that you're excited for us to pursue together in the future? Think long term here.

7.39 - Can you list three challenges you expect us to face in the future that worry you?

7.40 - Finally, can you suggest three (or more) strategies we might try to overcome those challenges as a team?

This is a good point to take a little break and check in with yourself. How are you feeling about these answers? Did you notice any similarities in your future personal plans and your collective plans? Or did you find that your partner's next few steps are heading in a different direction than you expected?

Neither reality is a foolproof recipe for success or disaster. If you noted lots of differences, you might want to have a purposeful conversation with your partner to figure out how you can make space for both of your visions in the relationship.

If your goals are already quite similar, you might want to talk instead about how your relationship will fare if these goals suddenly become unreachable--for instance, if a large percentage of your focus is on building a family together, how might your relationship handle a struggle with infertility or inability to adopt?

Furthermore, in the case that your goals are already aligned, you will each need to make a concerted effort to hold onto your own identities within the relationship. As a society, we tend to romanticize relationships wherein couples spend all of their time together, know each other inside and out, and each partner feels like they could not live without the other, but in reality, these are not healthy ideals to strive for. It's reasonable to perform selfless acts from time to time and make small personal sacrifices to build something great together, but without healthy boundaries, you could easily give too much of yourself to your relationship, and wind up feeling drained or neglected.

If this is a concern of yours, each of you should review your answers from the first set of questions in this chapter, and determine some firm boundaries for yourselves.

For your own benefit, list at least three personal values or goals that you would not be willing to give up, even if your partner pressured you to. If you or your partner has a difficult time recognizing the difference between your personal needs and the needs of the relationship, then professional counseling might be a healthy next step.

Remember, setting boundaries is not the same thing as being stubborn or emotionally closed off, insisting on full autonomy or focusing exclusively on your own needs. In any relationship, total independence can be a barrier to intimacy. As you grow to trust one another, it's natural to begin relying on each other for certain things. For example, in a committed relationship, one partner might volunteer to take care of cooking meals if their loved one lacks kitchen skills, or is often busy with work late into the evenings; meanwhile, the other partner might agree to pay for the groceries, or handle the dishwashing after the meal. You might grow to count on your partner in larger ways, too: for emotional support in times of difficulty, or for physical support when you are injured or ill. It's also natural to be somewhat flexible about your boundaries, allowing firm rules to be bent under extreme or fluctuating circumstances.

Healthy couples function interdependently. There is a vast difference between being co-dependent and interdependent.

A person who is co-dependent in a relationship may struggle to maintain personal friendships outside the partnership, to identify personal feelings or desires, and have trouble standing up for their own needs if they clash with the needs of their significant other. If you find that you are prioritizing the needs of the relationship over your own well-being, this is a sign that your relationship has become codependent to an unhealthy degree, and you'll want to take some steps to restore balance in the partnership.

A person who has mastered interdependence is comfortable trusting their partner to accommodate some of their needs, but he/she also has a support system in place outside of the relationship. They are able to take time and space away from the relationship without feeling the stability of the relationship might be threatened, and they feel secure in knowing that their personal needs are just as important as the needs of their partner while striving towards collective happiness.

For your partnership to stand the test of time, you'll need to build a strong support system for it. Work to find a balance between shared and independent recreation time. Both of you will need to pursue your own hobbies and passions. It is wise for each of you to have your own friends to turn to in times of need, or when you simply want to blow off some steam. If you plan to share a business, child, or other time-consuming responsibility, make sure that both of you are compromising equally for it, and that you each are given opportunities to take time away from this responsibility.

Maintaining the Self in a Partnership

This last exercise poses only a handful of questions, but they are deep ones. I'd recommend that you give yourself at least ten minutes to ponder it on your own.

This subject might be painful to think about, but try to remember this is just a hypothetical.

7.41 - Imagine that your significant other has suddenly disappeared--passed away or left the picture for some other reason. What would you do with all the time they once filled? (Note: "dating" is not a productive response here--we're aiming to focus on the self, outside of any romantic attachments)

7.42 - Would you make any major changes to your lifestyle?

7.43 - Eat at a different time?

7.44 - Sleep differently?

7.45 - Move to a different climate?

7.46 - Change your career?

7.47 - Spend time with different friends or family?

7.48 – What parts of your life together would you maintain, even in your partner's absence?

7.49 – What parts of your routine would you be happy to let go of?

7.50 – Think of the goals you outlined together earlier in this chapter. Would you feel well-equipped to continue striving for them on your own?

Chapter 8

The "Touchy" Questions

Sometimes, it's difficult to discuss issues with our significant others, no matter how safe we feel with them or how deeply we trust them. Issues that are deeply ingrained in your identity, like your ethnicity, socioeconomic background, spiritual beliefs, and political leanings can be tough to talk about with your partner, even if you fundamentally agree on them and respect each other's values. Matters of personal sensitivity, like traumatic past experiences, life choices for your future, or matters of self-esteem, can also be particularly difficult to talk about, even after you've become well- versed in all the healthy communication ground rules reviewed in chapter 1. Why is that you can talk to your partner easily about your greatest fears and deepest desires, but when it's time to talk about losing weight, personal finances, the challenges of monogamy, or whether or not you're ready to have kids, a simple conversation starts to feel like a mad dash through a minefield?

Some factors can steer any conversation off the rails, but these sensitive topics tend to get us all riled because we take them too personally.

It's easier to illustrate with trivial subjects: if you and your partner fundamentally disagree about the merits (or lack thereof) to be found in the color orange, you're not likely to see your partner's opinion on color as a reflection of your worth as a person. Somehow, though, when the matter at hand is even mildly related to our bodies, minds, social or financial standing, we all seem to have a much harder time noting the distinction.

Communication Guidelines for Ideological Disputes

Sometimes, the best course of action is to avoid a topic that you know you can't agree on, like steering your car around a pothole in the road. But if your ideologies are closely related to your career, or other daily experiences, it may not be possible to avoid the subject forever.

Whether your views are polar opposites or mostly aligned, here are some foolproof tips for talking about your ideological identity with your significant other:

- Accept early on that you will not likely be able to change your partner's mind.

- Try to discuss rather than debate whenever possible. You can look for common ground in your ideologies, and work to understand each other's perspectives rather than trying to negate or disprove one another's beliefs.

- If you absolutely must debate, stick to facts, not feelings.

- Always be respectful and remember your communication ground rules.

- Even if you feel you have good reason to be skeptical, listen when your partner speaks.

- No mocking, interrupting, and/or dismissing each other's statements.

- End the conversation on a positive note so that neither person will carry unresolved anger through the rest of the day.

Personal Sensitivities

What about difficult issues that are more grounded in our concrete realities--our bodies, our finances, our health or social standing? We all have our own unique sensitivity issues--things that other people might not mind talking about, yet when they come up in our conversations, we react as though someone is pressing the edge of a razor blade against a raw nerve.

For some of us, it might be weight or body image that's hard to talk about; or, it might be a circumstance which we have even less control over, like a health condition sustained since birth, or a permanent injury. You might find that your partner has a sore spot when it comes to discussing their financial insolvency, a broken relationship with a family member, or anything that even slightly reminds them of past trauma.

The last thing you want to do is aggravate an already sore spot, so if it isn't necessary to deal with the issue straight away, leave it up to your partner to determine when, where, and how you discuss it. One way to open the door for a discussion like this is to tell your partner you'd like to talk but on their terms. Encourage the discussion as a way to improve your relationship together, rather than as a hurdle they must clear on their own to please you.

You might say: "I love that we've been sharing so much with each other lately, and I want that to continue. But I've noticed you seem uncomfortable whenever X topic comes up. I'd really love to know what you're thinking about X, but I don't want to push you. Would you be willing to try and talk about it with me sometime? And will you let me know if there's anything I could do to make the conversation easier?"

Now, what if there is some degree of urgency, and you feel you cannot afford to leave it in your partner's hands? Say, for instance, that you've noticed your partner gaining a significant amount of weight. You still love them, but since they've gained this weight so rapidly, you're concerned for their health and too worried just to wait it out. How could you bring this to your partner's attention without causing strife in the relationship?

First, you'll want to set the mood, as described in chapter 2; prepare yourself and your partner for the conversation you want to have, not the argument you fear. Arrange a time to talk face-to-face, without any pressure to rush or concern of being overheard.

Second, you may want to approach the subject slowly; if you dive into the topic immediately, your partner may feel ambushed and try to shut down or run away.

Third, highlight the reason for your particular concern by reminding your partner how much you care for them. You might explicitly state that you are not angry, and they are not in trouble with you—when a person is feeling sensitive, these things may not be patently obvious to them.

Fourth, it helps to envelop criticisms in compliments; offer a positive first, then touch on your concern, and finish up with another positive.

Fifth, keep the conversation on topic; a defensive partner is likely to try and distract you or change the subject to shift focus from the sensitive issue. Don't engage with replies that sound like this: "But what about your problem with X? Isn't that just as bad?" If your partner does this, you might reply: "We can absolutely discuss that at a later point, but right now, I'd like for us to stay focused on you until we can resolve this issue."

Finally, don't rush it. If this is an issue your partner can barely say three words about without squirming, then you're not likely to find a solution after one hour of deep conversation. Set smaller goals for a series of shorter discussions: your goal for the first may simply be to get comfortable talking about it, while your goal for the second might be to brainstorm solutions and then talk about implementing them in

a third discussion. Change takes time, so don't go into the discussion expecting to see miraculous transformation overnight.

The Broken Record

One issue that couples commonly face is the degradation of trust when one or both parties fail to honor promises they've made. When the broken promise means a major betrayal--infidelity, for example-- lots of work will need to be done to rebuild trust. But if the broken promises are relatively small, and the trouble really lies in the frequency of their occurrence rather than their severity, the simplest solution is to stop making promises so lightly. Perhaps your partner over-promises their ability to contribute financially, or arrive places on time. If there's a repeated pattern of promising, failing to meet the expectation, apologizing, and promising again, the promises and apologies start to lose their meaning, and the issue becomes a touchy subject for both partners. The person making (and breaking) the promises may start to struggle with feelings of inadequacy or incompetence whenever the matter is brought up, while the other person may start to worry that they aren't being listened to or valued in the relationship.

Stop the cycle of empty promises. It will be better for the relationship if both parties admit this is a problem area, and that thus far, one partner hasn't been able to remedy the problem on their own. Instead, it might make more sense for both partners to come up with a new strategy to combat the problem together, as a team. Focus on the real obstacles that are preventing one partner from honoring this promise, rather than blaming the failure on a lack of effort or consideration.

The "Touchy" Questions

It's great to know how to approach difficult subjects, but how can you use these tools if you don't know what your partner is sensitive about? For some of the issues mentioned above, like religious views, body image or financial standing, it's fair to assume that most people are sensitive and that the conversation should be handled delicately. But your significant other isn't most people, and understanding their sensitivities will make it much easier for you to be a supportive partner.

Create a safe, calm space together without sources of external stress; make sure you won't be rushed; keep phones, tablets, and all media screens turned off or out of sight. Secure a piece of paper and writing utensil for each of you. When you are both comfortable, use as few or as many of these questions as you'd like to try and get a feel for each other's sensitive spots.

Answers don't have to be given in depth. The purpose of this exercise is to find each other's sore spots, not to pick at them. Use your paper to mark the questions that seemed especially tough for your partner, and when you're done, you might share your guesses and provide feedback on each other's accuracy.

You might also take note of your partner's body language and verbal tone; often, we proclaim that we are comfortable while our eyes, hands, or feet are practically screaming "get me out of here!" It could be useful to take some notes for your own benefit, recording what you notice about your partner's reactions. When a touchy subject is raised, do their shoulders get stiff? Do they blink more or less rapidly? Can they maintain eye contact? Does their voice or speed of speech fluctuate? Do they become jittery?

There's no need to call these behaviors out--simply take note of them so that you can better recognize your partner's anxiety and

discomfort in the future.

8.1 - How do you feel about your body size and shape?

8.2 - How do you feel about your physical ability?

8.3 - How do you feel about your capabilities as a (future or potential) parent?

8.4 - Money should never be discussed in polite company--do you agree with this statement, or not?

8.5 - What do you really think of monogamy in modern life? (If your views on the concept don't necessarily reflect your wishes for this relationship, make this clear in your response)

8.6 - What about honesty? Do you believe it's ever acceptable to lie? If so, under what circumstances?

8.7 - Do you find it easy or difficult to get along with people whose religious views don't align with your own?

8.8   - What about political views?

8.9   - How do you feel about your racial or ethnic identity?

8.10 – Would you say you feel secure or insecure in your social standing?

8.11 – Are you comfortable discussing sexual issues with friends in graphic detail?

8.12 – What about mental health concerns? Would you feel comfortable reaching out to someone if you were feeling depressed? What about if a friend reached out to you for support?

8.13 – How important would you say your financial status is to your identity?

8.14 – Do you think it's appropriate to judge another person's vices or bad habits?

Putting Theory into Practice

The last exercise we'll do in this chapter has only one question. There's no need to use pen and paper here. The only goal you have in this exercise is to use your communication ground rules, as well as the concepts suggested for ideological discussions at the start of this chapter, to talk about parenthood.

Let me repeat that: you will simply talk about parenthood. You don't have to make any decisions about it at all.

If you and your partner haven't yet discussed or decided on this issue, it will be uncomfortable, probably because you both know that the decision to procreate (or not) has come between a lot of otherwise compatible couples. Realize that discomfort is just a feeling, and it will pass. If your views are in contrast, don't overreact

—remember that they already were disparate, and all that has changed is that you've articulated them aloud. It's better to open up a discussion about an issue like this with purpose and patience than to have it come up as an accident or ultimatum.

If parenthood is old news to you and your partner, I'd still encourage you to use this exercise, but choose a different touchy topic, like personal finance.

8.15 – Can we discuss the one subject we've been most anxious to avoid, and stick to our communication ground rules?

Moving Forward

Of course, the point of any relationship isn't simply to work your way through a series of tough conversations--so why are we doing all of this?

Ultimately, your goal is to move through disagreements and difficult discussions in such a way that your relationship lands in a better place than it was beforehand. When both partners feel able to confront difficult issues together, that means they feel secure enough to be emotionally vulnerable in the relationship; this, in essence, is the key to fulfilling intimacy, both emotional and physical.

A lot of us struggle with vulnerability because it involves risk. When we are honest and open about our imperfections, there is always a chance we'll be answered with mocking; when we admit to our fears, there is always a chance they will be exploited; when we pursue the things or people we want, there is always a possibility that we will fail or be rejected. While this fear might be hardwired into your nervous system, working through conflict and discomfort as a couple can help you retrain your body to feel relaxed and open in your partner's presence.

As humans, we are drawn to authenticity and comforted by the vulnerability in others. You might believe that your partner wants to find perfection or infallibility in you, but research shows that we prefer to spend time in the company of those who admit to weaknesses and let us see their imperfections. Why? Because around them, we feel we can finally exhale, and admit our own weaknesses and imperfections, too. When two partners are able to be vulnerable together, it creates an ideal environment for either of them to take chances, try new things, grow as individuals and deepen the bond between them.

If you've done all the exercises in the previous chapters, then hopefully that's where you are right now. Congratulations, and welcome to intimacy! I hope you'll stay here for a long while.

Chapter 9

The "Touchy Feely" Questions

Now that you and your partner have cleared the air, don't you just feel like you're on cloud nine? Do you feel like the two of you could overcome any challenge together now, no matter how steep?

You probably could--but that doesn't mean you should. Not right now, at least. If you worked through some difficult issues in the last few chapters, you should give yourselves a little break. It's well deserved after all the relationship work you've done. Pat yourselves on the back, and go bask in one another's company for a while. You can always return to earlier chapters and work through more of your issues in a week or two.

When you've reached a place of deep trust and connection with your partner, there's no reason not to dive in deep and enjoy your emotional intimacy right away. Emotional intimacy is not a fixed thing; in any relationship, it can ebb and flow, rising and falling like the tide, so enjoy the water whenever the tide is high!

You can establish and maintain emotional intimacy by keeping yourself open and vulnerable with your partner and doing your best to create an environment wherein your partner can feel comfortable doing the same. If you reach a point where the intimacy becomes so strong that you feel you know your partner inside and out, like the back of your hand, remember that people can always surprise you. Keep asking questions and trying new things together; or, you might make a point to spend some time apart, and then come back together with new perspectives to share with each other.

Enjoying Emotional Intimacy

You know you love each other... but how do you share your love and get the most enjoyment out of it? Answer these questions together, and if any of them inspire you to take a break for a physical expression of love, go right ahead and indulge yourselves.

9.1 - What would you say is your favorite thing about our relationship?

9.2 - Can you name three current realities of our relationship for which you are grateful?

9.3 - What is one aspect of my personality that you truly appreciate?

9.4 - Since we've known each other, what aspect of your life has most improved?

9.5 - Aside from telling you how much I admire you verbally, can you list three things I do in our relationship that help you to feel loved and appreciated?

9.6 - Can you list three things that you do to express your love for me that you wouldn't do for anyone else?

9.7 - Is there a song that you already consider to be our song? If not, what song should we choose?

9.8   - Can you describe a point when you felt especially proud of our partnership?

9.9   – Do you remember the first time you wanted to say "I love you" to me? What inspired that feeling?

9.10 – In what ways do you think we make each other better people?

Improving Physical Intimacy

Physical intimacy in your relationship is about a whole lot more than just sensual pleasure. A desire for sexual connection may be the initial basis of many relationships, but it's certainly not the only type of physical intimacy that matters. Whether you've been physically intimate for years, have yet to cross that threshold, or have grown distant after a fight, there is never a better time to focus on your physical connection than right now. After you've reconnected, allowed yourself be vulnerable, and worked through a challenging issue together, you're in the perfect position for a tender touch to have the most impact on your mutual affection and personal self-esteem.

As humans, we crave comforting touch in all forms--this desire is so deeply ingrained in our psyches that infants who are deprived of comforting touch in their formative months can actually stop growing as if they're being starved. Yes, really! So no matter how much life gets in the way, you must make an effort to get physically connected with your partner when the time is right, and stay that way for as long as you can to keep your spark alive and sizzling.

If you're worried about coming on too strong, remember to build up gradually to intimate acts. Start with gentle, casual touches and leave some time during which you can see if your partner is receptive and willing to engage with you.

If there is any room for confusion at all, remember to ask for consent and wait for an enthusiastic, positive response before ascending new levels of physical intimacy with your partner.

For physical touch inside and outside the bedroom, it's always best to tell your partner what you want, react positively to touches you enjoy, and never fake it just to stroke each other's egos. Remember, authenticity paired with vulnerability is what we're most drawn to. Be honest, be yourself, and be willing to listen to requests or suggestions without being defensive.

If all else fails, sit down with your partner outside of the bedroom, and try to have a rational discussion about your physical intimacy. What's working? What isn't? What new things can you try? The conversation might make you blush or feel a little exposed, but in the long run, it will pay off, and you'll be glad you had it.

Chapter 10

Maintaining the Magic

Now that you've gone through all these questions, I wish I could tell you that the hard work is over--that, as in a fairy tale, a ribbon banner would spread out over your heads once you close this book cover, declaring you ready to move forward together, "happily ever after." But alas, there's plenty of disparity between love in fairy tales and love in real life, and the idea that "'happily ever after' actually exists" might be the most dangerous lesson to take away from such stories.

We can't be too hard on ourselves for buying into this myth. It's not only in children's stories that we find unrealistic pictures of true love and what it ought to look like--namely, that once we've found it and made a commitment to it, all the hard work is over, and the light switch of happiness should remain in the "on" position forever more. As adults, we find this concept in romantic comedy movies, in novels, in games, in song lyrics. The idea is central to modern wedding culture. You might even recognize it in the way that companies design work-life balance for employees. You're expected to get time off for a wedding, honeymoon, or new baby, but who asks their boss for a week off to prevent a marriage from crumbling?

Modern culture often tries to teach us that finding and securing love is what life is all about when in reality, it's less than half the battle.

Relationships are like gardens; you can't just plant seeds, water the area a few times, and then expect it to self-maintain. You'll need to keep the water coming and make sure nothing blocks the sunlight. Weeds will sprout up from time to time, and you'll need to root them out. Your relationship is like a living organism-- like a pet, it will never stop needing to be fed or nurtured. But the more consistently you nourish it with time and attention, the easier it will be to maintain its health in the long run.

As your relationship matures, a lot of the excitement you feel for it may start to settle. One way to ensure this fading excitement, which is due to a lack of novelty rather than a change in the feelings you harbor for your partner, is to adopt the habit of regularly trying new activities, imbuing your relationship with refreshed energy.

You might want to carve out a few minutes here and now to brainstorm some new activities to try as a couple. Use the prompts and below to come up with some ideas. Write them down and post them on the refrigerator door, or type them into an email chain so both of you can access the list and add new suggestions as they come to you. There's no such thing as too many ideas here; if you've made it this far through the book, chances are your love is built to last, and you two may find yourselves with a great deal of time to kill together in the future.

Brainstorming New Activities Together

The first step is to drum up some enthusiasm! Try to get yourself back into the "miracle" mindset of chapter five, when you talked about your visions for the future without letting yourself feel too weighed down or discouraged by the challenges you'd face in real life. Start by thinking big, as though there are no limits at all to what you two could accomplish together, and have fun with your suggestions.

10.1 - Would you want to visit a new country together? Where, specifically?

10.2 - What kinds of climates, historical landmarks, or other attractions get you most excited?

10.3 - What about physical feats? Extreme sports adventures, scuba diving, swing dance lessons, tandem yoga? Remember to hold onto an anything-is-possible mentality here.

10.4 - How about creative skills you've always wanted to hone? Cooking, crafting, painting, woodwork, writing, sculpture?

10.5 - Would you enjoy a deeper connection with the natural world? Any interest in camping trips, nature retreats, a trip to a national park or wildlife refuge?

10.6 - Or if you'd rather stay closer to home, perhaps planting a garden, or keeping bees would be a fun new adventure?

10.7 - Do you enjoy large projects? Is there something grand and long-term you can see yourselves working to build together?

You might re-decorate a room or an entire home from top to bottom; design an item or invention, and see it through to fruition; start an organization, company or meeting group; plan a party or other major event together.

10.8 - What about giving back? Are there issues that you've always felt passionate about and wanted to be more involved in, but could never find the time? Charity work, community organizing, political fundraising, child mentorship programs?

Big suggestions shouldn't be ruled out or put down simply because they're big. While some of the suggestions you and your partner make might seem extreme and unrealistic at first, you could find that there isn't much stopping you from pursuing these activities as a team besides fear and habit.

Don't rule these ideas out, but for now, let's set them aside. Write down the big ideas with some notation, like an asterisk, and come back to them whenever you're ready for a big change.

For now, though, you'll want to translate these ideas into a list of activities you could really try out tonight, this weekend, or next month.

First, try to dial some of your most outlandish ideas down a bit. In what ways could you make these activities more accessible? If one of you suggested a trip around the world, for instance, could you really work to make this happen? Or might it still be fun for you to scale your ambitions back a little and plan a round-the-world food and culture tour in your own hometown? If you suggested climbing

Mount Everest, could you still manage to get your kicks by climbing a smaller mountain that's closer to home?

You might have some physical or financial limitations that stymy your enthusiasm during this brainstorming session. Try to stay focused on the positive possibilities, and remember that your partner is on your team. If money is tight and preventing you from pursuing the new activities that interest you, perhaps you and your partner can think of a new activity to do together that will help you to raise extra money. It may not sound terribly glamorous to suggest that you clean out the basement and organize a yard sale together, but there are plenty of ways to make the project fun: blast music, play a word game, enjoy your favorite snacks, take breaks, and keep your goal in mind if the task ever starts to feel daunting. The sense of collective accomplishment you'll feel when it's over will be a reward in its own right, and it will be good for both of you two know that you can solve problems cooperatively.

Here are some more prompts to help you create a list of exciting--but still accessible--activities. Keep this list handy and force yourselves to try new things at least once a week moving forward.

10.9 - An easy place to start is in your own neighborhood. Are there any local restaurants or businesses that you'd like to try out? Centers for adult education that offer classes? Recreation centers that host parties and events?

10.10 - Are there any new skills you'd like to learn that you could feasibly acquire without taking a class? For example, using web tutorial videos, you might learn how to whip up a perfect creme brûlée; you might use books or recorded tapes to learn a new language together.

10.11 - What about skills that one partner could teach the other? If so, remember to keep this focused on fun, as an exchange of information between two equals. Condescension and criticism are never good for any relationship.

10.12 - What are some simple and easy ways you could shake up your routine? Excessive screen time is problematic for lots of couples, leaving them to feel disconnected and distant even as they sit side by side; maybe you can agree on a designated daily time frame during which screen time is forbidden.

10.13 - Do you ever find yourself struggling to relax? Maybe you could try meditation, yoga or tai chi. You might exchange massages, or find other ways to pamper one another without ever having to spend a single dollar at the spa.

10.14 - Is there anything new you'd like to try in your physical relationship? Remember this can be a "touchy" subject, so adhere to communication ground rules and be respectful of your partner's feelings.

Get Your Heart Racing

Adrenaline can be an extremely useful tool to keep your relationship invigorated and full of fresh energy. Our brains tend to draw connections everywhere, even in places where they shouldn't; this means that we associate our emotions with the people that are present when we experience them, whether or not they're responsible for any of the circumstances that drive these feelings. So if you attend a comedy show with a date, you might remember that date as being funny, even if the only words they say to you all night long are: "take a seat." On the other hand, if you encounter a certain person repeatedly in stressful situations, you might come to regard that person as a source of stress.

Together with your partner, choose an activity that sets your heart racing. Perhaps this means riding a roller coaster, going skinny dipping, performing at a karaoke bar, sky-diving, or signing up for dance classes.

When you do these things, you are tricking your brain; essentially, you're putting butterflies in your own stomach and training yourself to associate the feeling with your partner. That may seem disappointing or inauthentic to you, but remember that the sensation of butterflies in your stomach is really a sign of anxiety early in the relationship. We feel the butterflies because we are not yet certain the love will last, and the unpredictability makes us nervous.

A long-term relationship with solid commitment doesn't leave either partner much room to fear losing their love so it may be better to manufacture thrills, rather than to create true instability to accomplish the feeling.

You can also create this feeling by supporting one another as you pursue independent thrills. Suppose your partner has always wanted to go cave diving, but the thought of small enclosed spaces makes

you feel panicked. You can still help encourage your partner to seek out this adrenaline rush on their own. You can show interest and support as they are training and preparing, asking questions and attentively listening as they express their excitement or anxiety. Be a motivational coach, and your partner's number one cheerleader. Imagine an actor accepting an academy award, pointing to their spouse from the podium on stage and gushing: "You worked just as hard for this as I did--this award really should have been given to you!"

Aim to inspire that reaction in your partner. They will never forget it.

What about you, though? You don't necessarily need to court danger to find an adrenaline boost. Is there anything that you've always been curious about, or wanted to try, but never allowed yourself to explore due to a fear of failure or judgment? Maybe the idea of public speaking sets your heart racing or the thought of finally submitting that short story you wrote for publication makes your stomach flip. Talk to your partner about it and jot down a few ideas for a rainy day. Sometimes, the act of simply declaring a goal aloud can make it feel more real and accessible, whereas silent rumination can lead us to feel overwhelmed and incapable.

If your partner has been reluctant to get the ball rolling with new activities, then you may want to take it upon yourself to do some thrill-seeking on your own. There's no need to wait for their support or permission to get started (though ideally, support should come soon thereafter) and your actions may inspire your partner to take more initiative on their end. You may even find yourselves engaged in a healthy competitive dynamic. So long as you both feel supported and respected, there's nothing wrong with a little competition between you; it can be a powerful motivator for growth, and help to keep your relationship full of forwarding momentum.

"What makes us work?"

Here's a quick activity that you can use to maintain an appreciation for your differences. You can complete it together or separately; however, you feel it serves you best--but if you do it alone, keep your answers close at hand in your memory so you can share these thoughts with your partner in opportune moments. Remember that it's never a bad time to tell your partner how deeply you value the bond you share together.

10.15 - List three things you have in common that you enjoy sharing.

10.16 - List three differences you have that sometimes cause problems for you.

10.17 - Now, list three things you have in common that pose a challenge to the success of your relationship. (A few examples: we are both too stubborn to find our way to the end of a disagreement; we are both disorganized; neither one of us is satisfied with our career.)

10.18 - List three differences between you that allow you to be stronger as a team.

10.19 - List three areas of your relationship that you'd like to see improve or change. Note: this isn't an opportunity to sling blame or criticism at each other-- you're looking for areas wherein you could both do better.

10.20 - Finally, list three aspects of our relationship that you hope will never change.

Creating a Connection Ritual

No matter how young or old your relationship is, it's never a bad idea to get into this habit. You'll have to get into the practice of making time for each other if you want to thrive as a couple, no matter how unnecessary it may seem in the present moment. Sooner or later, life will throw distractions at you that test the strength of your bond. Remember closeness doesn't happen by accident, but if you establish a daily or weekly ritual to focus on your connection, you'll be much less likely to wake up one day and suddenly find that you've drifted apart.

Here are some prompts to help you design a personalized connection ritual, followed by a few examples of what you might do to get started. Remember every relationship is unique, though, so you may find more success by brainstorming together and creating your own ritual.

10.21 - What time of the day or week do we have the freest time together?

10.22 - Do we currently spend a good deal of that time distracted by media (phone/tv/reading/games), chores or work?

10.23 - If so, is there a way we could easily compartmentalize that time? Are we willing to give up some media time or make a point of finishing chores in the morning so the evenings can be kept free?

10.24 - What makes us feel most connected? Talking? Touching? Enjoying a shared experience?

10.25 - If we had no limitations on time, travel, or finances, what would be a dream date for us?

10.26 - Can we find a way to translate the essence of that experience into something we can recreate at home, in just a few hours? As an example: if your dream date was dinner and dancing at your favorite New York City steakhouse, you might try to cook a similarly festive meal at home together, and then clear the furniture to the edges of your living room to create a makeshift dance floor.

10.27 - Do we share any interests or hobbies that we can't discuss with friends, family or colleagues?

10.28 - If so, how might we carve out a regular chunk of time to discuss this interest with each other, and make sure it's something we both can look forward to?

Below, you'll find some examples of connection rituals. Some are more time consuming than others; some require specific timing, atmosphere, or props to complete, while others can be performed anytime, anywhere, with nothing more than your bodies and minds. Try not to let yourself feel anxious if none of these sound like a good fit for your lifestyle; remember, every couple is unique, so there is no right or wrong way to do this.

You may want to try working your way down the list, giving each ritual a trial week before evaluating how well it works for you. Listen to your gut--you know your relationship better than any therapist (or book author) ever will, so you can be the judge. Feel free to alter or edit these rituals; make them simpler or more in-depth, quicker or longer-lasting, depending on what your relationship needs at this stage.

Also, remember that it's normal to feel awkward the first time you enact any of these rituals. The activities might feel forced, stiff, or inauthentic. Try to stick it out and work through the discomfort, at least once, and see if it gets easier the second or third time around. There's no need to keep banging your head against an unrelenting wall, though; if you've tried a ritual for a week or more without any improved sense of connection, recognize that it isn't working for you, and move on until you find a ritual that feels right.

The lazy morning ritual

Agree to wake up twenty-thirty minutes earlier than you normally would for work. Spend the extra time lazing together--enjoy a warm beverage, read the newspaper, go for a relaxing stroll outside, or stay in bed to snuggle a while longer before you face the day. This can help you both to feel connected, supported, and calm as you head into a busy day apart.

Passing notes

A simple and easy way to bring more positivity and connection to your relationship is to write each other love notes. Leave them in your partner's pocket or work bag, or post them on the mirror or a kitchen appliance. These notes could be simple explanations of how you feel about your partner; they could feature an invitation to a date or fun activity, a creative little love poem, an inside joke or a fond memory. You might just write a note of encouragement before your partner heads into a challenging day, or a list of compliments. This might be especially beneficial for those who struggle to express their feelings verbally.

Relationship check-in

Oftentimes, the best way to prevent frustration from becoming a major problem in the relationship is to get your feelings off of your chest before they have the chance to fester and sow resentment. Some couples find it useful to schedule an hour (or more) once a week that is designated for both partners to air their grievances. You

might even come to this hour prepared with a list of topics that you want to discuss. It can be particularly effective in compartmentalizing household chores and life responsibilities, keeping these issues separate from the love, trust, and attraction that comprise the foundation of your relationship.

Say you're over the moon for your partner's personality and looks, but they consistently leave their dirty socks on the floor. After weeks, months, or years of this behavior, you might be understandably peeved--but is this worth ending your relationship over? Is it worth the effort of micromanagement, nagging your partner every single time they take off their socks, and potentially creating a sore spot in the relationship? Sometimes, you might find that all you need to do is express all your anger, frustration or confusion before you're able to take a deep breath and accept that this is just who your partner is.

This ritual is meant to help you move into your next week together with a clean slate; the goal is to leave your negative thoughts and feelings behind once the check-in is over. It's important to recognize that this hour isn't designated for arguing; if there is too much back- and-forth, the activity will not be productive. Instead, set a timer to allow each person five to ten uninterrupted minutes of speech before switching off. When your partner has the floor, refrain from judgment or negation; just try to listen. If you're both using your communication ground rules and "I feel" statements, there shouldn't be any need to interrupt or correct each other.

Make sure you end the check-in on a positive note. You might set aside the last ten minutes to suggest resolutions or plans to handle things differently moving forward. If not, be sure to express gratitude to your partner at least before you end the session. A sincere "thank you for listening," can go a long way.

Personal check-in

If you find it easier to deal with conflicts at the moment and don't have enough unspoken frustrations to fill up an hour-long check-in session, you might find this quicker alternative to be more useful. Rather than airing grievances, you can use a check-in to simply get better attuned to what your partner is feeling today, in this very moment, whether it's something positive, negative, or just plain confusing.

Sit or stand facing each other so that you can easily maintain eye contact. Establish a physical connection by holding hands, or if you're sitting, you can intertwine your legs to get closer to one another. Looking into each other's eyes, take a few deep breaths until your inhalations and exhalations are in sync.

Once you feel calm, safe, and fully attentive with each other, you can begin taking turns asking the following questions of each other and answering as honestly as possible.

"How are you feeling right now?"

"How are you feeling about yourself today?"

"How are you feeling about our relationship today?"

"Are there any fears or concerns on your mind right now? If so, can you tell me about them?"

"What are you most looking forward to right now, in the near or distant future?"

"Is there anything I could do today to help support you?"

You may find yourself articulating personal feelings to your partner that you previously did not recognize inside yourself. This practice is a form of mindfulness--you may be surprised at what comes up, but whatever happens, remember to be accepting of each other's feelings (and of your own).

Again, it's a good idea to wrap up this ritual with an expression of gratitude. Thank your partner for giving you their undivided attention, and share a hug or kiss before moving on from the exercise.

Trust exercises

Most of us are familiar with the typical trust-fall exercise. It's often used in corporate retreats, improvisational acting classes, and community building events. By this point, you may feel that falling backward and trusting your partner to catch you is too easy--you've been through so much together already, so a trust-fall would be a piece of cake! If this is the case, there are more elaborate trust exercises that can help strengthen your bond and set you both up for a good laugh.

Choose a fairly basic activity in your home--loading the wash, making a sandwich, organizing the closet--and take turns trying to accomplish the task with one person purposefully handicapped. You could wear a blindfold and have your partner verbally steer you through an obstacle course or simple chore. You might keep your hands tied behind your back and instruct your partner to complete a task that's normally yours to manage. Alternatively, you could each keep one hand behind your back and try to cook an omelet together with only two available hands between you both, like a grown-up version of a three-legged race, to challenge your ability to work as a team.

Remember to stay safe--blindfolds in the kitchen can be dangerous, and the point of this exercise is not for either of you to end up in the emergency room. Don't worry about impressing each other with your capabilities. The aim is to get silly and have fun, so if you're not laughing hard throughout this activity, you might need to choose a more challenging task.

Make each other smile

If you're looking for a ritual that can be performed quickly and without much in the way of resources, this might be a good fit for you. Initially, each person will have to think of one thing their partner does that can always make them grin or laugh, without fail. This should be

something that both partners find amusing and are comfortable with, not something that allows one person to laugh at the other's shame, embarrassment or humiliation. A signature funny face or inside joke reference would fit the bill perfectly.

Whenever you two are about to split up for the day (or longer) exchange these gestures before you go, trying to elicit a genuine smile from your partner. This way, at any given time that you are apart, your most recent memory of your partner will be a happy one.

Conclusion

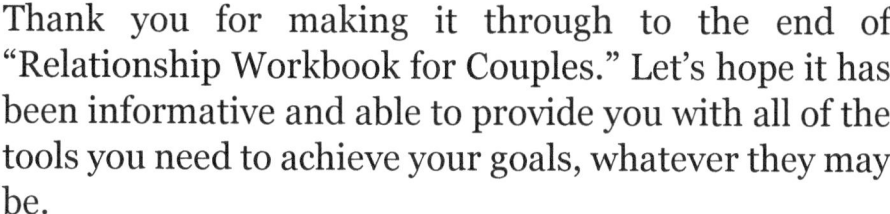

Thank you for making it through to the end of "Relationship Workbook for Couples." Let's hope it has been informative and able to provide you with all of the tools you need to achieve your goals, whatever they may be.

Even though you've completed these exercises and learned a lot about yourself, your partner, and the unique bond you share, relationship work is never complete. It's important that you both embrace and continue to practice what you've learned in these pages to keep your love thriving for years to come. We truly do get back what we put into our relationships, and they require constant, continuous effort to stay healthy. You should close this book cover knowing that there will never come a point at which you can say that you know all there is to know about your partner, or that you've contributed enough for the relationship to self-sustain hereafter.

On the contrary; if you've reached a point where you are no longer willing to put in the effort to evolve with your partner, it may mean the relationship is no longer serving either of you, and it is time to contemplate your attachment to each other seriously.

However, I am hopeful that your completion of this workbook is a good sign for your future together. Working through it as a team shows a high degree of desire, dedication, and commitment to the relationship. Regardless of your compatibility—whether you like the same colors, foods, movies, music, hobbies or friends—the health of your relationship will ultimately be determined by your willingness to invest in its future success.

Whether you do it on your own or in the office of a qualified couples' counselor, continue to nurture curiosity in yourself and your partner. Keep asking questions, and let yourself be open to unexpected answers. Do not set this book down and expect happiness to find

you—pursue your happiness actively, hand-in-hand. If you don't yet know what that happiness will look like or where to find it, go on asking questions until the pathway forward begins to look clear.

With the foundation of love, trust, and curiosity you've built together, you are sure to find your way.

www.ingramcontent.com/pod-product-compliance
Lightning Source LLC
Chambersburg PA
CBHW071625080526
44588CB00010B/1277